The Grief They Don't Talk About: Losing a Cat

How to Find Peace Again

C. S. Sterling

Foreword by Ben A. Collingstone

Table Of Contents

Foreword

by Ben A. Collingstone

Grief has a way of surprising us.

It doesn't always arrive in the places we expect or follow the rules we were taught about what should and shouldn't matter. Sometimes, it enters quietly... carried on soft paws, woven into daily routines, tucked into the ordinary moments we never thought twice about.

And then one day, those moments are gone.

For those who have loved a cat, you already understand something the world doesn't always say out loud: this kind of loss is real.

It is not small.
It is not silly.
It is not something to rush past or explain away.

It is love... with nowhere to go.

Cats have a unique way of choosing us. They are not always loud in their affection, but they are steady. Present. Observant. They sit beside us in silence, curl into our lives without asking permission, and somehow become part of the rhythm of our days. And when that rhythm breaks, the silence can feel overwhelming.

You may find yourself reaching for them without thinking. Listening for sounds that no longer come. Noticing the spaces they used to fill in ways you never noticed before. That is not weakness. That is love, still moving.

This book does not try to fix your grief, because grief is not something broken. It is something carried. Something honored. Something that reflects the depth of what you shared. What you will find in these pages is permission.

- Permission to feel the loss without minimizing it.
- Permission to remember without rushing forward.
- Permission to hold onto the love without feeling like you need to let it go.

Because love does not end when a life does.

It changes form. It becomes quieter, perhaps... but also deeper in ways we don't always understand right away. If you are holding this book, it likely means you are in that quiet space now. And while no words can fully remove that ache, I hope these pages remind you of something steady and true:

You did not imagine the bond.
You did not over feel the loss.
And you are not alone in carrying it.

Take your time here.

There is no hurry through love.

— Ben A. Collingstone

Introduction

The house felt different after my cat died. There was a stillness that was heavy, as if the air itself understood something precious was missing. I kept expecting to hear the tiny thud of paws on the floor, the soft meow at the door, or the quiet weight of a warm body pressed against my leg at night. But the silence was sharp. It cut through my days, reminding me again and again that my companion was gone.

If you are reading these words, chances are you know this pain too. Maybe you're in the thick of it, questioning every decision, wondering if you did enough or if you waited too long. Maybe you are just beginning to feel the ache. Or perhaps you carry the loss quietly, tucked away in your heart where others can't see.

I wrote this book because I have been there. I am still there, sometimes. The loss of a cat is different from any other loss I have known. I don't say that lightly. Cats slip into our hearts in their own way, sometimes quietly, sometimes with a force that surprises us. They weave themselves into our routines, our moods, our sense of home. When they leave, the world changes shape.

For me, writing this book is both a way to honour my own beloved cats and to reach out to others who are hurting. I know how lonely this grief can feel. Society doesn't always understand. Friends might tell you to "just get another cat" or that "it's only a pet." But you and I know that isn't true. The bond you shared was real, and so is the grief.

If you feel isolated or misunderstood in your pain, please know you're not alone. I see you. I see the love and the loss. I see the questions that keep you up at night and the longing that stays long after others think you should have "moved on." There is nothing small or silly about the love between a person and their cat. Our grief deserves space and compassion.

This book isn't about offering empty comfort or clichés. I promise you won't find advice to "just think positive" or to "keep busy." Instead, you'll find practical guidance drawn from my own experience and from the stories of others who have walked this path. Together, we'll explore ways to process guilt, regret, and doubt. We'll talk about honouring your cat's memory, handling the difficult days, and finding meaning in your grief.

Inside, you'll find chapters dedicated to the different stages of loss. We'll look at guilt, anger, and sadness, as well as love, gratitude, and hope. There are simple exercises and gentle suggestions, space for reflection, and real stories from people just like you. Some chapters will offer advice for talking with friends and family who don't understand. Others focus on rituals and creative ways to keep your cat's memory alive.

No two people grieve the same way. Your loss is unique, and so is your journey. Whether your cat was with you for a few months or many years, whether the goodbye was sudden or expected, whether you feel relief, heartbreak, or both, your feelings are valid. This book welcomes all of them. There is no right or wrong way to grieve.

My hope is that you will find comfort here, and maybe even moments of peace. I want to help you answer that hard question: "Did I do the right thing?" I want you to know that you're not alone in asking it, and that kindness, to yourself most of all, is part of the healing.

As you turn these pages, I invite you to take the next step with me. Let's walk through this together, one small moment at a time. Let's honour the love you shared, the choices you made, and the journey you are on now. Your story matters. Your cat's story matters. And the path to peace, though it may twist and turn, is one worth taking.

You're here. That's enough.

Before we begin, I want to define some new terms that you will see throughout the book.

Meowmories

The sweet memories of your cat that return unexpectedly, like remembering the sound of their paws in the hallway or the way they curled beside you at night. Meowmories can bring both smiles and tears, reminding you how deeply your cat was loved.

Whisker Memories

Tiny, everyday moments you shared with your cat that stay with you long after they're gone, such as their whiskers brushing your hand, their curious nose inspecting everything, or the way they watched the world from the window.

Purr Therapy

The quiet comfort that comes from remembering the soothing presence of a cat's purr. Even after a cat has passed, thinking about those peaceful moments can calm the heart and bring a sense of warmth and reassurance.

Phantom Meows

The strange but common experience of thinking you hear your cat after they're gone, perhaps a faint meow, the sound of paws, or a soft rustle.

These moments happen because your mind and heart are still used to your cat being part of everyday life.

Grief Waves

The natural ups and downs of mourning a beloved pet. Some moments feel calm, while others bring sudden sadness when something reminds you of your cat. Like waves in the ocean, these feelings rise and fall as healing slowly takes place.

Chapter 1

WHEN LOSS HITS HOME: UNDERSTANDING
YOUR UNIQUE BOND

THERE ARE MOMENTS WHEN YOUR CAT'S ABSENCE FEELS almost physical, the air seems heavier, your chest tightens as you pass their favourite windowsill. After saying goodbye, you might still reach for a mug and almost call your cat's name to offer a splash of milk. It's these small routines that linger the most: the morning coffee with your companion basking in the sun, or the cosy evenings with a warm, purring presence curled in your lap. After a loss, these simple moments take on a bittersweet gravity, reminding you how deeply your cat was woven into your daily life.

Why Losing a Cat Hurts So Much & Honouring the Human-Feline Bond

THE BOND YOU SHARE WITH YOUR CAT IS UNIQUE. IT'S ABOUT MORE than petting soft fur or hearing purrs. There's a silent language, a whole vocabulary of glances, slow blinks, and gentle kneading paws. Cats learn to read your moods, comforting you when you need it or giving you space during quiet moments. A steady purr can soothe worries or sadness in a way words never could. This "purr therapy" brings real comfort, a type of healing only a cat can give.

This intimacy is hard to explain to someone who hasn't felt it. You might call yourself a "cat parent," and it's not just a joke. For many, their cat is their chosen family, a confidant, a silent therapist, or a steady friend, always there. When you call them your "fur baby," it reflects a connection filled with trust and affection. Cats don't care about your appearance or mood; they simply show up every day, in their own way.

Daily routines deepen this bond. Maybe you started the day with coffee by the window, your cat stretching while you watched the birds together. Maybe your evenings ended with "zoomies" across the living room, little rituals that became emotional anchors, giving shape and stability to your days. When these vanish, the sense of loss can feel overwhelming, because you're missing more than a cat; you're missing the pieces of your life that formed around them.

Cats are more than companions; they're witnesses to our quietest, most vulnerable moments. In times of loneliness or sorrow, your cat would simply sit alongside you, offering silent comfort. Unlike human relationships, which can get tangled in expectations and conversation, a cat's presence is a gentle acceptance.

Grieving a cat is real and valid, even if others don't understand. Studies show that human-animal bonds, especially with cats, can be as deep as any human relationship. If you're feeling profound loss, you're not alone; your emotions reflect the deep love and investment you gave to this bond.

This isn't "just" losing a pet; it's losing family. The world may downplay your pain, but the impact is real: routines have shifted, your home feels emptier, and your heart aches in surprising ways. Cats fill a space in our lives no one else can occupy.

If you keep replaying those shared moments, the purrs that comforted you, the head bumps that made you smile when nothing else could, you're honouring your bond. Those memories are proof of a connection built on trust and affection. Your intense grief is a reflection of how much your cat meant to you.

Reflection Section: Mapping Your Cat's Place in Your Life

Take a sheet of paper or open a document. List three routines or rituals that changed after your cat passed. What do these memories make you feel? Where do you most sense their absence? Allow yourself to feel it all, sadness, gratitude, anger, or anything else, as they are natural responses to honouring such a special bond.

Your pain is understandable and expected when love runs this deep. The bond with your cat was uniquely yours, rich in daily joys and quiet miracles. Your grief deserves space. The chapters ahead will explore ways to honour those memories and find peace in their absence.

"Just a Pet"? Society's Blind Spot and Why You're Not Overreacting

WHEN I TOLD A COWORKER MY CAT DIED, SHE PAUSED, OFFERED A weak smile, and changed the subject. No "I'm sorry," just an unspoken message: "Isn't it time to move on?" It stung. I ended up swallowing my feelings, wondering if I should have kept the news to myself. This is all too common. In many places, work, family gatherings, or casual chats, you're expected to quickly recover after losing a cat. People might say, "It was just a cat," or "You can always get another." These comments are rarely meant to be cruel, but they isolate you. Your grief feels unwelcome, as if you're being dramatic for grieving someone who didn't speak your language but meant the world to you.

You might hesitate to share your loss. Perhaps you've seen people's eyes glaze over when you mention your cat's name in the past tense. In these moments, a quiet shame creeps in, as if you're asking for too much. This is society's blind spot: our culture reserves grief for specific relationships. When your loss doesn't fit, people minimize it. What they miss is the depth of your bond—a daily companion, a reliable comfort, a friend with unwavering acceptance. Words like "It was only a pet," "At least it wasn't your child," or "Are you still upset?" can linger and hurt long after the conversation.

There's nothing trivial about what you're feeling. Reviews of pet loss books are filled with people saying, "No one around me understood why I was so heartbroken," or "My family rolled their eyes when I cried, " and " I felt totally alone." Others simply say, "I needed this book because everyone else acted like I was crazy." These aren't rare, they're the norm. Surveys and studies confirm that pet loss triggers real and lasting grief, especially if you saw your cat as family. This pain is a genuine response to losing someone irreplaceable.

So, what to do when others dismiss your feelings? First, trust your experience; your grief is real, no matter what anyone says. Here's your permission: you're allowed to mourn as deeply and as long as you need. You don't owe anyone an explanation. If others don't understand, that's not your problem. If someone says something minimising, it helps to have a response ready: "I appreciate your concern, but she was family to me," or "He mattered more than I can put into words." If you're caught off-guard, a simple "Thank you for listening, I'm just really missing her right now" can signal that your pain is real and ongoing.

If you're up to it, share a small detail about your cat to show the depth of your relationship. For example: "Every night she greeted me at the door no matter how my day went," or "She sat with me through my hardest times." These words aren't to persuade, they're for you, to affirm your feelings.

Remember: cultural attitudes aren't always right or fair. Grief doesn't need anyone else's approval. If you start to shrink or apologise for your mourning, recall how many others hide their heartbreak because they're told it "doesn't count." You're not too sensitive; you're simply being honest about your love.

When comments sting, it can help to have a few simple responses ready:

- "I know not everyone understands, but she was family to me."
- "It's been really hard. Thanks for being patient with me."
- "I'm grieving right now; I hope that makes sense."

If you need to be firmer: "This loss hit me harder than I expected," sets a boundary without inviting debate.

You have every right to honour your feelings. Don't let others measure your pain or rush your healing. Give yourself space to mourn without guilt; your heart deserves nothing less.

Whisker Memories: Celebrating the Tiny, Everyday Moments

But grief isn't only something we navigate with others; it often shows up when we're alone. Grief doesn't always announce itself with big, dramatic waves. More often, it creeps in through the smallest openings, quiet, unremarkable places where your cat's presence used to live. Maybe you're vacuuming, and you spot a stray whisker on the couch. Suddenly, your chest tightens. That single, silvery strand is proof of a life so recently interwoven with yours. It's such a small thing, but it hits you: she used to nap right there every afternoon, curled into the sunbeam like she owned the world. These little tokens carry enormous weight. The sound of paws padding down the hallway before dawn, the faint jingle of a collar in the next room, or the shadow that flickered under the door while you brushed your teeth, these are memories stitched into the fabric of your days. When they vanish, it's not just routines you lose; it's a sense of comfort and belonging that's hard to replace.

What really surprises most people is how much these micro-memories shape our sense of loss. It's not only the holidays or birthdays that sting; it's

Wednesday mornings when you pour cereal and look down to see no curious face peering up, hoping for a taste. Or Sunday afternoons, realizing you haven't laughed at your cat's strange "chirp-meow" in weeks. Cats are experts at inserting themselves into every corner of our lives, especially in all the subtle moments others might overlook. Their vocal quirks, maybe your cat had a deep yowl announcing his entrance, or a tiny squeak when he wanted attention, became a language just for you. I still hear phantom sounds from time to time, especially late at night. My mind fills in those "meowmories" where silence now sits. It's a strange mix of pain and comfort, realising how much life those sounds brought into my ordinary days.

The healing potential in these tiny details is real, even if it feels raw at first. Honouring them can become part of your grief process. Sometimes, I write down a memory as soon as it floats up, a silly antic, the way she stretched her front legs out like Superman, or that one time she tried to "help" with a puzzle by scattering pieces everywhere. Documenting these moments keeps my cat alive in my heart and gives me something beautiful to revisit when the ache flares up again. You might try starting a "whisker memory" journal, a safe place to jot down every small ritual or habit that made your bond special. It doesn't have to be neat or polished; scribbles on scrap paper or notes on your phone work just as well. These memories can become touchstones on harder days.

Sharing these little stories with someone who understands, maybe a friend who also loves cats, or an online group, can help lighten the heaviness inside you. I once posted a funny story about my cat's obsession with stealing socks in a pet loss forum. The replies overflowed with people sharing their own "sock thief" tales and laughing through tears with me. Suddenly, I didn't feel so alone in my grief. Sometimes a single shared memory brings comfort not only to you, but to others who miss their own companions just as fiercely.

Exercise: Honouring Your Cat's Everyday Magic

Grab a piece of paper or open a blank note on your phone. List five tiny rituals or habits you shared with your cat, maybe it was the morning stare-down for breakfast, or the way she squeezed herself into impossible boxes. How do these memories make you feel now? Write honestly, if it brings tears, let them come; if it sparks laughter, allow yourself that joy too. If you're up for it, pick one story and tell it to someone who will listen without judgment, a close friend, a family member, or someone online who gets it.

These moments matter. In honouring them, you honour the life you shared and the space your cat filled in your heart. The ache around these memories is sharp because their love was threaded through every ordinary day. Celebrating these small joys can be a gentle way to keep connection alive while also finding space to heal as you move forward together, with their memory beside you.

Your Cat's Forever Home & How You Changed Each Other's Lives

THINKING BACK TO THE DAY A CAT FIRST ENTERS YOUR LIFE IS LIKE opening a door to another time, a version of yourself you might barely recognise. Maybe it started with a photo online, a cage in an animal shelter, or a frightened pair of eyes peeking out from under a porch. You bent down, extended a hesitant hand, and something shifted. In that instant, two lives began to transform, yours and theirs. The story of a "forever home" is never just about rescue; it's about mutual discovery. You didn't just save your cat. Your cat, in return, rescued hidden parts of you.

For many, the early days test patience and hope. A nervous cat might hide for weeks, watching from shadows, unsure of this new world. You learned to move more slowly, to let trust build one blink at a time. Maybe you placed treats along a safe path or read aloud in the evenings so your voice would become familiar. Over time, the shy observer transformed, inching closer, until one day you realised you had gained a steadfast friend. That quiet breakthrough, the first purr, or the tentative leap onto your bed, felt like winning a small, silent lottery.

The impact isn't one-sided. Cats, too, carry scars, sometimes visible, often hidden. Your patience worked miracles. Maybe you navigated litterbox mishaps or soothed their trembling during thunderstorms. You learned to anticipate their quirks and fears, changing routines for an older cat or giving up sections of your home to make space for their comfort. Late-night vet visits became stories you tell with a mix of exhaustion and pride. Bottle feedings at 2 am or emergency runs when something seemed wrong taught you resilience and tenderness you never expected from yourself.

Being a "cat mom" or "cat dad" isn't just a cute title. It's a badge earned through acts of devotion, small and large. You became an advocate, fighting for your cat's health when others might have given up, researching every new symptom, learning to read subtle signs of distress or contentment. You rearranged furniture so arthritic paws could reach favorite perches. You learned to medicate with one hand while offering treats with the other. When they aged, you adjusted yet again, soft beds in sunbeams, extra patience with accidents or confusion. These acts might feel ordinary at the time, but looking back, they show how deeply you cared.

The timeline from first meeting to final goodbye is rarely smooth. There are rough patches: scratched arms from failed nail trims, shredded curtains, illnesses that seemed insurmountable. But alongside these hurdles come victories, celebrating "gotcha days," marking anniversaries with new toys or treats, or simply marvelling at how far your cat has come since those uncertain beginnings. Each year together stitched another layer of connection: the first time they accepted a new friend into the house, braved the terror of fireworks without hiding, or let out a rumbling purr during a storm because they trusted you to keep them safe.

Every relationship has imperfections, missed cues, moments when frustration won out over patience, times you wondered if you did enough. When loss arrives, those memories might haunt you with "what ifs." Did I notice that limp soon enough? Should I have taken her to the vet earlier? Did I say goodbye the right way? Let me offer this: love is not measured by flawlessness but by effort and intent. You gave your cat safety and comfort, shaped their days with affection and care. Even when you made mistakes or felt lost, you always came back to love.

You played every role your cat needed: caregiver, protector, playmate, nurse. You bore witness to their quirks and moods and met them with patience more often than not. The home you built together was a tapestry of shared habits and mutual understanding. Through every challenge and every small victory, both of you grew; your cat learned trust; you learned empathy and resilience.

If guilt still lingers in the corners of your heart, let me reassure you: your love was enough. Your effort mattered more than any misstep or missed sign. The life you gave your cat was filled with warmth and a sense of belonging, a true forever home. You didn't need to be perfect; you only needed to show up and care, which you did again and again. That is what endures above all else.

When Others Don't Understand: Navigating Alienation and Dismissal

Sometimes the sharpest sting of grief doesn't come from the loss itself, but from the echoing silence that greets you when you try to talk about it. It's a peculiar loneliness, the kind that settles in when you realise your sadness doesn't fit into the stories or sympathies others are willing to share. You might find yourself withdrawing from conversations, hesitating before mentioning your loss, or dreading the awkward pause after you say, "My cat died." There's an unspoken message in these moments: this isn't grief that "counts." Maybe at a family gathering, someone talks about losing a parent or partner, and you want to join in, but the second you say your loss was a pet, the mood shifts. You see polite nods or hear a quick subject change, as if your pain belongs in a different category, less real, less worthy of space. This feeling of exclusion is both common and deeply wounding. It can make you question your own feelings, as though loving your cat so fiercely must be a personal oddity. The isolation grows heavier when others don't acknowledge your loss at all, or worse, when they expect you to "bounce back" after only a few days. You may even stop mentioning your grief altogether, keeping it hidden because it feels safer than risking more misunderstanding.

There is nothing wrong with you for feeling this way. The loneliness of being misunderstood is real. So many cat owners walk this quiet road, doubting themselves because no one else seems to notice the empty spot at the foot of the bed or the hush that falls over the room at night. In some workplaces, people rally around a colleague who's lost a family member, sending cards and condolences. Yet when it comes to a beloved cat, you're lucky to get a brief nod or a passing "Sorry." Sometimes friends don't ask how you're doing at all. This lack of support can make your grief seem invisible. But invisible pain is still pain. It weighs just as much.

Finding validation can feel like searching for a lost item in a crowded room, difficult, but not impossible. One of the best ways to break the cycle of isolation is to seek out those who truly understand. Pet loss support groups exist for exactly this reason. These aren't just places for sharing tears; they're spaces where no one will ask you to justify your sadness. You'll meet others who nod in recognition at your stories and offer gentle understanding instead of impatient advice. Online cat memorial forums are another lifeline. In these spaces, strangers become companions in grief, offering compassion and empathy you might not find in your everyday circle. When I joined an online group, I was struck by how quickly my words found resonance; someone hundreds of miles away had felt the same pang seeing an empty food dish or hearing phantom meows in the quiet hours. The relief that comes from being seen cannot be underestimated.

It's also important to give yourself permission to set boundaries with those who don't understand. You do not have to explain or defend your grief to anyone who dismisses it. Practice saying things like, "I need some space right now," or, "This loss has hit me hard, and I'd rather not talk about it with people who can't relate." If someone keeps pushing or offers insensitive remarks, it's perfectly acceptable to walk away or change the subject yourself. Your emotional landscape belongs to you alone; you have every right to protect it.

Anecdotes from others who have faced alienation can help you see just how widespread this experience is. One person shared how her own brother rolled his eyes when she cried at dinner after her cat died; she stopped talking about her feelings for months afterwards. Another described how a coworker sent a quick email, just two lines, when her cat passed away, while other colleagues organised lunches for those grieving human relatives. And yet, connection is possible. A friend once told me his local bookstore owner quietly set out a sympathy card when she heard about his loss; he wept in gratitude because someone finally acknowledged his pain without minimising it.

You are not alone in this odd limbo between visible and invisible grief. Seeking out those who understand, even in small ways, can help rebuild trust in your feelings and soften the edges of isolation. Set your boundaries with confidence and know that protecting your heart is not selfish; it's survival. Your story deserves listeners who honour its weight, even if they're strangers on a screen or quiet supporters on the sidelines.

A Grief Like No Other & How Cat Loss Differs from Other Grief

Losing a cat leaves you wandering through a landscape of absence that doesn't look like any other form of grief. The shape of your days shifts in quiet, often invisible ways. When you lose a person, there is usually a structure to guide you, a funeral, family gatherings, and a formal reason to take time away from daily obligations. But when your cat dies, the world keeps moving. Emails pile up at work, dinner needs cooking, and most people around you don't even pause to notice that your world has tilted. There's no official ritual or ceremony to mark this kind of loss unless you create one for yourself. You don't get a few days off work to cry or remember. Your pain has to fit into the cracks between regular life, and that alone makes it harder to carry.

Evenings stretch longer and colder without the quiet company of a "lap buddy." That empty space where your cat used to curl up becomes a silent ache, a stark reminder that something precious is missing. No one else misses that warmth the way you do. The house feels quieter, but it's not just about missing a pet. It's about missing a rhythm, a presence that quietly shaped the flow of your home. The routines that once felt automatic, pouring kibble into a bowl, checking the window for a familiar face, become ghost movements, habits that no longer have meaning but refuse to disappear.

Cat loss is often "hidden grief." It happens in private. Most people don't see you sitting on the kitchen floor, cradling an old toy or holding back tears in the grocery store aisle because you saw their favorite treat. There are no casseroles delivered to your door. Friends rarely organise gatherings in memory of your cat. Instead, grief unfolds in solitude, behind closed doors or in those silent moments when you finally let yourself feel the full weight of what's gone. This privacy might seem easier at first, no need to explain, no need to mask your pain for others, but it can deepen the sense of isolation. Without shared acknowledgement, your loss can start to feel invisible even to yourself.

What makes losing a cat so distinct is how they defy easy labels in our lives. A cat can slip into the role of friend, child, therapist, and companion, all within a single afternoon. They listen without comment, judge nothing, and offer comfort in ways that are both subtle and profound. Maybe your cat greeted you at the door each day after work, making the transition from outside chaos to home feel soft and safe. Maybe they sat beside you through heartbreak, illness, or anxiety, offering only their steady presence as balm for your wounds. These are not just animal behaviours; they're acts of companionship that blur boundaries and create bonds few humans can match.

There's also a strange complexity in how we mourn cats compared to other losses. With people, relationships are usually defined as a parent, sibling, or partner. With cats, the connection is more fluid. Some days you're caretaker and protector; other days you're the one seeking reassurance from their gentle gaze or steady purr. The relationship is built on mutual need and unspoken understanding. When it ends, it's not just one role you lose, it's many at once: confidant, comforter, playmate, and family.

Because there is so little formal recognition for this kind of grief, it's easy to doubt yourself. You might wonder if you're overreacting or if your sadness makes sense. I want to say clearly: your loss is valid in all its complexity. You are allowed to mourn in ways that feel right for you, even if those ways don't look like anyone else's process. If your grief feels strange or more intense than expected, that's not a sign of weakness; it's a sign of real connection.

You don't have to fit anyone else's definition of what loss "should" look like. Your experience is yours alone, shaped by every shared glance and quiet night together, and it deserves every bit of acknowledgement you need to give it. If you find yourself searching for rituals or ways to honour your cat's memory, know that this is both normal and healing. Lighting a candle at dusk or keeping their photo nearby can be powerful acts of remembrance, even if no one else witnesses them.

Grief after losing a cat may be private and unspoken by those around you, but it holds just as much depth as any other sorrow. If the world doesn't make space for your pain, make space for yourself, lean into your memories, honour your emotions without shame, and let yourself remember just how much this connection meant. The silence left behind is proof that something irreplaceable was there, something worth grieving fully and without apology.

When the days feel especially long or the nights seem colder than before, remind yourself that this pain is not proof of weakness but a testament to love's enduring reach. In honouring what was lost, you keep alive everything beautiful about what you shared, quietly, honestly, and on your own terms.

Chapter 2

Grief Waves & Why Some Days Are Harder Than Others

GRIEF IS A STRANGE COMPANION. ONE DAY, YOU WAKE UP AND almost feel like yourself again, maybe you even catch yourself smiling at a memory, thinking the worst is behind you. Then, without warning, it crashes back. Maybe it's during a routine drive, where you suddenly find your eyes stinging with tears just because the sunlight hits the dashboard in a certain way, reminding you of your cat's favorite napping spot. Or you're walking through the grocery store and a particular scent, a bag of treats, the earthy whiff of catnip, floods your chest with longing so intense you have to pause in the aisle and steady yourself against the cart. These are what I call "grief waves." They arrive out of nowhere, washing over you with a force that can feel almost physical, leaving you breathless and raw.

The unpredictable nature of these waves is both unsettling and completely normal. You might go days or even weeks feeling steady, then suddenly get knocked sideways by a memory or a sound. It's not just the big anniversaries or obvious reminders; sometimes it's as tiny as hearing the soft rustle of a plastic bag or feeling the warmth of the sun through a window. This ebb and flow is not a sign that you're failing at grief or that you're not "moving on" fast enough. You might think you're finally healing, then get swept away by sadness all over again. This is normal.

What makes these grief waves so tricky is how they sneak up even after long stretches of stability. You may start to believe you've turned a corner, only to have a setback that feels as intense as those early days. This can be discouraging. You might even question your own strength or sanity, wondering why you can't just "get over it." But those setbacks are not failures. They are reminders of the love you shared and how deeply your cat was woven into your daily life. Even after the sharpest pain fades, love leaves an imprint, and that's why these waves can rise up long after you thought they'd passed.

When one of these days hits hard, it helps to reach for practical tools. First, pause and notice your breath. Take three slow inhales through your nose, hold each breath for a few seconds, then let it out gently through your mouth. This tiny act can anchor you when the wave feels overwhelming, giving your body something steady to hold onto. If possible, retreat to a "grief-friendly" space at home, a corner with soft blankets and maybe a photo of your cat or a favorite toy kept nearby for comfort. Allow yourself to sit with the feeling instead of pushing it away; resisting often makes it stronger.

Another approach is to gently narrate what's happening inside you: "I'm having a tough moment right now because I miss my cat." Naming your experience helps separate you from the wave itself, making it feel less like drowning and more like riding something that will eventually pass. If you're at work or in public when grief hits, excuse yourself, even if just for a minute. Splash water on your face, breathe deeply, and remind yourself that this intensity won't last forever.

Reflection Exercise: Tracking Your Emotional Tides

Consider starting a simple mood tracker or journal for a few weeks. Each evening, rate your day with a color or number that matches how heavy or light your heart felt, maybe use blue for tough days, yellow for okay days, green for lighter ones. Over time, patterns may emerge: perhaps Mondays are harder because that was your "cat and coffee" morning;

maybe certain seasons sting more than others. Visualising your emotions doesn't make them vanish, but it can help you spot triggers and plan ahead for rough patches. Some people use apps with mood-tracking features; others keep an old-fashioned calendar and add coloured dots or simple notes ("cried while folding laundry," "felt okay until bedtime"). This isn't about controlling grief but about understanding its rhythms so you can ride out the hardest days with more self-compassion.

Looking back on my own colour-coded weeks after loss, I saw that those hardest days often followed periods where I'd been busy or distracted, almost as if my mind waited until I slowed down to let the sadness in. If you notice similar patterns, don't judge yourself harshly. The waves are not punishment or proof that you're stuck; they're part of loving deeply and living honestly with loss. When a grief wave hits next time, remember: this is normal, this is loving, and this too will pass.

Phantom Meows and Empty Food Bowls: Daily Triggers and How to Cope

GRIEF OFTEN SNEAKS INTO ORDINARY MOMENTS. YOU MIGHT FIND yourself unconsciously reaching for the food bowl in the morning or pausing to listen for the phantom meow that should greet you at sunrise. These small, daily habits sting not because they're dramatic, but because they remind you of what your "normal" once was. You may glance at your favorite chair, expecting to spot a twitching tail, or catch yourself leaving out a bit of food as you always did for your little beggar under the table. The pain is sharpest in these daily routines: the empty bed corner, dusty toys, and the strange quiet at mealtimes.

Your mind adapts slowly after loss. Even months later, you may expect to see your cat sneak through the hallway or leap onto your lap. This is more than nostalgia; it's the residue of years spent following routines together. Familiar cues, footsteps, collar jingles, the thump of a cat landing, simply vanish, so your senses try to fill the void. Some people experience fleeting sounds or sensations so vivid they force a double-take. Others catch themselves performing old rituals like filling a water dish or calling a name at the door. These reflexes persist because love, routine, and memory are deeply connected.

It can feel strange, or even embarrassing, to find yourself setting aside time or space for someone who's no longer there. You might wonder why such habits remain or why the sight of their favorite blanket still tightens your chest. The answer is simple: these triggers show how deeply your cat was woven into the fabric of your daily life. There's no shame in stumbling over these invisible reminders; they are proof of just how much space your companion occupied in your world.

Coping demands both kindness and creativity. One gentle strategy is to transform triggers into something new. For example, repurposing a cat's food bowl as a planter by the kitchen window can turn the pain into a gentler remembrance: each morning, watering the plant becomes a small act of honouring their memory. Some people keep a photo on their nightstand where their cat used to sleep, making it part of a new nightly ritual, a whispered "good night" to a memory rather than a living friend.

Others gather favorite toys, collars, or blankets into a memory box stored somewhere special. One reader filled her cat's bowl with river stones collected during walks they used to take together, each stone a reminder of a happy day. Another lit a candle at mealtimes for a week after her cat's passing, using the glow as a moment to reflect on what those meals shared meant to her.

If the emptiness in certain spots becomes overwhelming, try temporarily filling the space with something comforting. Place a soft pillow where your cat likes to curl up and use it as a journaling spot, or put a potted plant on the windowsill once reserved for bird-watching. Life goes on there, too.

Not every trigger can be reworked right away. Sometimes it helps to simply acknowledge it out loud: "I reached for her bowl again today, I miss her." Naming your experience reduces its surprise and allows you to process it more gently. If you share your home with others who love your cat, talk about these lingering triggers together. You might discover they're tripped up by the same moments.

Many have found comfort in sharing these stories online. For example, someone once posted that she kept hearing her cat's "goodnight chirp" in the evenings, and dozens replied with similar stories of phantom paw steps or reaching out for an invisible presence on the sofa. Realising you're not alone in these experiences offers solace; these daily aches are common for anyone who has loved deeply.

Sometimes, you may even laugh at yourself for leaving space on the couch out of habit, or catch yourself scolding an empty chair. Other days, the pain hits fresh. Both reactions are normal as you adjust your routines to life without your feline friend. Every small adaptation is a form of self-care, and each memory you choose to honour keeps their love present in your everyday life, even if it now looks a little different.

"Am I Losing My Mind?"— Understanding Sensory Grief Experiences

After your cat is gone, your body and mind often play tricks on you. Late at night, you might feel the familiar dip in the mattress from your cat leaping up beside you, or catch a glimpse of movement in the corner of your eye and, for a moment, believe it's your cat. These moments can be vivid and real, prompting you to reach out or call their name before you remember the truth. You might wonder if you're losing your mind, but these experiences are normal; they're a common part of mourning.

There's a scientific reason behind these sensations. Years spent with your cat wire your brain to expect their presence, as you learn their patterns and movements. Even after they're gone, your brain's neural pathways remain ready to respond to familiar cues. This is your mind's way of holding on to important connections, not a sign of losing touch with reality[1].

Sensory grief may show up in different forms. Some people hear faint meows from another room or the jingle of a collar. Others notice a scratch on a door that hasn't moved. Personally, I would sometimes hear a soft thud behind me while reading, my heart leaping before I remembered. These encounters can bring comfort, a fleeting sense that your cat is nearby, a reminder of the love still lingering in your home. Sometimes these moments bring peace, as if your cat is watching over you. On quieter days, they serve as gentle reminders that your memories are very much alive.

However, these experiences can also trigger anxiety or confusion. You may feel unsettled by how real the sensations are, or worry that you're stuck in grief. Embarrassment or fear of being judged can sometimes prevent you from sharing these experiences. Whether you feel comforted or distressed, both responses are valid. How you interpret and respond matters most; sensory grief isn't about seeing ghosts, but about your brain and heart working together to process loss.

When these sensations happen, gentle self-talk is helpful. Remind yourself, "It's okay, this is just my mind holding on to something important." If you feel startled or overwhelmed, try to ground yourself: look for five things you can see, four you can touch, three you can hear, two

---

1. American Academy of Child and Adolescent Psychiatry. (n.d.). *When a pet dies.*

you can smell, and one you can taste. This exercise anchors you in the present and helps you process the experience without shame.

You might also comfort yourself in advance with kind phrases, like "This is just love taking shape as memory," or "I'm not broken, my heart remembers." If these moments are comforting, allow them without judgment; if they cause distress, remind yourself they are temporary and part of your healing.

Creative outlets can also help you process sensory grief. Try sketching the scene where you felt your cat's presence, or write in a journal or voice memo describing what happened, how it reminded you of your cat, and what emotions surfaced afterwards. Sharing these stories with others can lighten your burden, and sometimes simply saying, "I could have sworn she was right there on the windowsill," brings comfort or even shared laughter with someone who understands.

Talking to a trusted friend or family member can also help. There's often more understanding than you expect. Many people grieving pets have similar stories of phantom whiskers or soft purrs in a quiet house. Giving yourself permission to process these moments through art, conversation, or writing creates space for healing rather than fear.

Some days, it might feel as if these sensory reminders will never stop. Other times, they may fade for weeks before returning unexpectedly. This is normal. Your senses spent years learning to recognise your cat's presence; letting go takes both emotional and physical adjustment. Your mind is working through change at its own pace, turning memories into part of your daily life, so that love remains even after your cat is gone.

Sudden vs. Expected Loss: Processing Different Grief Journeys

There's no way to prepare for the first day you wake up, and your cat is simply gone, but how the end comes changes everything about what follows. Losing a young or healthy cat to an accident or acute illness is a punch in the gut. Shock sits heavy on your chest. The world goes blurry, time slows, and reality just won't stick. You might find yourself checking the door or glancing at the window, half-expecting a furry face to appear, refusing to believe what you know. There's anger, too, sometimes at fate, sometimes at yourself, sometimes at whatever circumstances snatched them away. For many, the mind starts a reel of "what ifs"—What if I'd shut that window? What if I'd noticed something sooner? The pain of a life cut short is sharp and raw; regret can gnaw at every memory, making even happy moments ache. You may feel robbed of years you thought you'd have, a future that evaporated without warning.

On the other hand, watching a senior cat grow frail or caring for a pet through chronic illness brings another kind of heartache. Grief starts before the actual loss, creeping in as you notice subtle changes: the way they hesitate at the stairs, how they sleep more, eat less, or lose interest in favorite games. You might spend weeks or months bracing for the end, measuring every good day against the bad ones, quietly preparing to say goodbye each time you leave the house. This anticipation can feel both like a gift and a curse. It gives you space to shower them with extra love, say what matters, and savour each little bit of time left. But it also fills every day with tension, a background hum of sorrow and dread that drains your energy. By the time the end arrives, you may feel both shattered and relieved, grateful for your years together yet worn out from carrying so much worry.

Both types of loss are valid; neither is easier or harder, they're just different kinds of pain. It's common to catch yourself comparing your grief to others', or even to your own past losses, but this only adds unnecessary weight to what you're already carrying. If your cat died suddenly, you might envy those who had time to prepare; if you said goodbye after a long decline, you might wish it had been easier or quicker. These thoughts are natural, but try not to judge yourself for them. Your heart doesn't know how it "should" feel—it just hurts because love was real.

No matter how the loss happens, many people find themselves wrestling with something deeper. As these moments settle in, many people begin to notice something else. Regret takes on different shapes depending on how you lost your cat. Sudden loss comes with relentless "if only" thoughts—if only I'd taken her to the vet right away, if only I'd been home, if only I'd seen the danger. The mind clings to tiny decisions, replaying them endlessly as though one small change could have rewritten fate. These thoughts can become exhausting and brutal. For those who witnessed a long decline, regret may sound like Did I wait too long? Was I selfish to hope for one more good day? Could I have given more comfort? In both situations, guilt and second-guessing love to set up shop and stay awhile.

To soothe these regrets, it helps to remember that love often means making decisions in the dark, guided only by your best intentions. No one gets a script or a guarantee. If your loss was sudden, consider creating a tribute that honours not just what was lost but also what was shared—a photo collage celebrating silly moments, or planting a tree in your cat's name so life can continue even after an abrupt goodbye. Sometimes writing a letter to your cat expressing all you wish you'd said brings relief; pour out your apologies, your anger at fate, and your gratitude for every stolen second.

If your goodbye was slow and expected, a different ritual might feel right. Many people find comfort in writing a "thank you" letter to their older cat, listing memories, lessons learned, and ways their cat changed their life for the better. Lighting a candle each year on the anniversary of their passing can transform dread into remembrance. Some people create a scrapbook chronicling the journey from kittenhood through old age, honouring each stage rather than mourning it alone.

No matter how your cat left this world, your grief belongs to you alone, messy, complicated, sometimes contradictory. There is no timeline or correct way to process loss; there is only love trying to find a way forward in a world that feels dimmer without your companion.

When Guilt and Regret Take Over—The "Did I Do Enough?" Trap

Guilt after losing a cat can settle like a heavy stone, surfacing in quiet moments and replaying every decision from the final days. People agonise over the timing of euthanasia, missed symptoms, or postponed vet appointments, and even recall times they were too tired to play or moments of impatience. Suddenly, every small misstep is proof they failed their friend when it mattered most.

This self-blame always circles back to "Did I do enough?"—a trap that catches even the most loving cat parents. The mind searches for evidence, replaying choices and moments, looking for neglect or errors. You may think, "If only I'd noticed that limp sooner," or, "Why didn't I push for more tests?" Even though you know logically that you did your best, your heart feels otherwise. These feelings are sharpest around end-of-life choices. Choosing euthanasia is both an act of mercy and a source of overwhelming doubt. No matter the reassurance from professionals or friends, the ache of "what if" lingers.

These feelings are so intense because as caregivers, we often take on responsibility that feels absolute. When a cat depends on you for everything, it's easy to believe their well-being is entirely in your hands. If something goes wrong, guilt creeps in, whispering that you should have known more, done more, or loved harder. But illness in cats is often stealthy and unpredictable; many conditions only become visible when they're advanced. Even vets say cats are adept at hiding pain, so it's impossible to catch every sign or control every outcome.

I think of a friend who, after her cat died from kidney failure, replayed every appointment and medication, searching for where she may have gone wrong. Nights involved scouring old records and photos, haunted by the question of whether a different choice could have given her cat more time. When her vet shared stories of other cats with sudden declines, it helped her recognise that sometimes, even the best care isn't enough. Knowing this didn't erase her pain but softened her guilt. Stories from professionals remind us that love sometimes means accepting our limits.

Guilt is less about what really happened and more about how much you cared. These feelings of self-blame reflect your devotion, not any failing as a caregiver. The "Did I do enough?" question is painful precisely because love always wishes to do more, but love's true measure isn't perfection; it's presence and effort.

To start letting go of regret, you don't have to forget. Instead, try shifting your relationship to those memories. For me, an exercise that helped was writing a letter from my cat's perspective. I'd sit quietly and imagine what she would say to my anxious heart: "Thank you for the warm windowsills, for listening to my purrs when you were exhausted. I forgive your distracted days and moments of fear." Writing those words brought tears, but gradually softened my harsh inner voice.

You might also try self-forgiveness exercises:

- Put your hand on your heart, close your eyes, and say (or write), "I did the best I could with what I knew and felt at the time."
- Remind yourself, "Caring means making hard choices without all the answers."
- Write a letter of apology and forgiveness to yourself, naming both regrets and things you did right.

- Promise to honor your cat's memory by treating yourself with the same kindness you gave them.

Loss inevitably brings regrets and questions. Guilt lingers in silence, but bringing it into the open is the first step to release. Talking with others who've faced these choices helps; a simple reminder that you're not alone may be enough to begin healing. Every loving act matters, even if things weren't perfect. Your cat knew your love far more than any missed sign or mistake.

Mixed Emotions: Laughter, Anger, and Relief in Grief

LOSING YOUR CAT IS NOT JUST ABOUT SADNESS, DESPITE WHAT THE world might say. There's a broad range of emotions that surface, unexpected and sometimes unwelcome. You may feel anger at losing your cat too soon or at everyday life continuing as if nothing happened. You might laugh at memories of your cat's wild antics, even during the funeral or while sorting through photos. Relief can also wash over you when you realise your cat is no longer suffering; watching their decline was its own private pain. Every emotion is real and deserves space.

Grief is never simple. It doesn't follow a tidy path. A flash of joy may come when you recall the time your cat knocked a cereal box onto the kitchen floor, spilling milk everywhere. That laughter is not a betrayal; it's your love resurfacing. Moments later, however, guilt may appear. "How can I laugh while mourning?" But grief is complex. Tears don't tell the whole story. Anger also emerges, not just at the loss, but at the unfairness of illness or accident, or your own powerlessness. Sometimes it points outward, at the world, and sometimes inwards, making you feel lost now that your cat is gone.

Relief is another complex feeling. When a cat has suffered through illness or the effects of age, saying goodbye can bring peace. You may feel lighter, even as you grieve. This relief doesn't mean your love was less; it means you truly wished for your cat's comfort, even if that meant letting go. Heartbreak and gratitude can coexist, grateful that their pain has ended, yet longing for their presence. If you sense relief alongside sorrow, honour that feeling. It is compassion for both your cat and yourself.

These emotions often bring confusion. Society's narrow expectations around loss rarely prepare us for laughter breaking into sadness, or light moments during mourning. Sometimes you might feel guilty for enjoying something or returning to an old hobby. The inner voice may ask, "If I laugh or move forward, am I forgetting?" The answer: absolutely not. Feeling joy, or any emotion, while grieving doesn't erase your love or loss. It proves your heart is still open, holding many feelings at once.

Make room for every emotion. Don't limit yourself to just sadness. Honouring your whole experience is healthy and healing. Notice when laughter, anger, or relief arises. If you remember how your cat used to hide in the laundry basket and find yourself laughing, note the moment, write a sentence, sketch a doodle, or snap a photo of something that reminds you of them.

Talking with a friend who knew your cat can also reveal layered emotions. Tears may give way to giggles as you reminisce about your cat helping with a puzzle by scattering the pieces. Sharing these stories connects you to others and keeps your cat's spirit alive through joy and sorrow alike.

If you're unsure where to start with your feelings, try prompts like:

- Write about a time your cat made you laugh until you cried.

- Recall a moment when anger surprised you after their loss.

- Describe what relief felt like as their pain ended.

- List three emotions you felt today and what sparked each.

Art is another outlet. Sketch a favorite silly pose or paint colors that match your heart's mood, whatever helps you process. There's no right or wrong way, just expression.

Permitting each emotion its place is an act of self-kindness and honours your cat's memory. They brought frustration and comfort, chaos and delight, all those feelings fused together are real love.

As this chapter ends, remember: grief is not just sorrow. It is everything love leaves behind: joy, anger, relief, laughter, pain, all intertwined. The next chapter will explore how these emotions shape daily life and how you can gently build new routines and memories while honouring the past.

Chapter 3

The Last Vet Visit: Coping with Medical Decisions and Euthanasia

Eventually, grief often asks for a moment of acknowledgement. There's a particular kind of dread that settles in your chest when you know the last vet visit is coming. It's a strange, heavy day where the world outside seems to keep spinning as usual, while inside your own skin, everything feels tense and fragile. You might replay every moment from the night before, remembering the way your cat rested against you or the slow blink they offered as if to say, "I trust you." Walking into the clinic, that familiar sterile smell hits, a mixture of antiseptic, faint animal musk, and a quiet that is both too loud and too empty. The waiting room feels like purgatory. Other pets come and go, but your mind can only focus on your cat's breathing, their soft fur beneath your hand, and the way time seems to crawl along, each second stretching into its own eternity.

Paperwork arrives, and with it comes a weight that's hard to describe. Signing those forms feels like crossing a line you never wanted to approach. Your hands might shake. Maybe you have to pause and steady your breath before you can even hold the pen. Each signature is another step toward goodbye, another moment of responsibility pressed into your heart. No matter how clear the vet's explanations are, everything feels hazy, like you're floating above yourself, watching this moment unfold but unable to change it.

When you know this visit is likely to be your last together, there are a few practical steps that can help you advocate for your cat and for yourself. If you can, bring something from home, a favorite blanket, a small toy, or even a T-shirt that smells like you. The softness and scent provide familiar comfort in a space that feels anything but safe. Ask your vet about sedation options before euthanasia; many clinics will offer a calming shot first so your cat can relax in your arms before the final medication is given. Don't hesitate to request extra time in the room, both before and after. Let the staff know whether you want privacy or prefer their gentle support nearby.

Prepare questions in advance, if possible. Write them down so you don't forget in the flood of emotion. What will the process look like? Can I hold my cat through it? How long does it take? Is there a way to make this gentler for her? Your voice might tremble; that's okay. Speaking up for your cat's comfort is an act of love. It's also fine to ask about logistics: what happens afterwards, options for cremation or taking your cat home, and how long you can stay with them after they've passed. Many clinics are used to these requests and will do their best to honour what matters most to you.

Even if you plan every detail with care, self-doubt often creeps in once everything is over. After a loss, your mind replays decisions: Was it too soon? Did I wait too long? Should I have tried one more treatment? This second-guessing is normal; it's how love tries to bargain with loss. Remember that veterinary teams see this every day; most people wrestle with uncertainty after saying goodbye. Even when you know intellectually that you made the best choice for your cat's comfort, the heart keeps asking questions.

You may also feel trauma from the experience itself; the sounds, sights, and final breaths can linger painfully in memory. If images replay in your mind or if you feel numb after leaving the clinic, know this is not unusual. Processing these moments takes time and kindness toward yourself.

Reflection Section: Gentle Self-Compassion Exercise for After the Vet Visit

Find a quiet space at home where you feel safe. Sit comfortably, letting your hands rest on your lap or over your heart. Close your eyes if that feels helpful. Take a slow breath in through your nose, hold for three seconds, then release gently through your mouth. Picture yourself sitting beside a younger friend who has just lost their beloved cat. Imagine what words you would offer them: soft encouragement, forgiveness, or reassurance that they did everything they could out of love. Now speak those same words quietly to yourself: "I did my best with what I knew at the time. My choices were made from care and compassion, not neglect." Stay here as long as needed, allowing any tears or emotions to rise and pass without judgment.

If guilt returns later or memories become sharp again, repeat this exercise as often as needed. You are not alone in these feelings; every loving cat parent wrestles with doubt after making hard choices. Allowing yourself this small ritual of self-forgiveness is not just kind, it's necessary for healing.

If it helps, keep a small token from that last visit, a collar, a tuft of fur, or even just the memory of your cat's final slow blink, as proof that love guided every step you took, even on the hardest day.

Writing a Goodbye Letter to Your Cat: A Guided Ritual

Putting pen to paper and writing a goodbye letter to your cat might feel daunting at first. Yet, this simple act can help give shape to feelings that swirl in your chest, love, gratitude, regret, even anger or relief. When I sat down with a blank sheet, unsure what to write, I was surprised by a flood of memories and emotions that rose up. The process didn't require perfect words or flawless sentences. Instead, it invited honesty. Letter writing is more than a sentimental gesture; it's a therapeutic ritual that allows you to speak the words you may never have managed to say out loud. It creates a space for your grief, and honours the bond you and your cat built over years, days, or even a brief but intense time together.

Start your letter with the words that come most naturally. "Dear Whiskers, thank you for every purr you shared when I was sad…" or "Sweet Luna, you changed my world with your gentle head bumps and midnight zoomies." Let your heart lead the way. Don't worry about grammar or handwriting. This is for you and your cat, no one else. Reflect on favorite moments—maybe the way they blinked lazily in the sunlight, the mischievous chaos of a sudden leap onto the counter, their comforting presence on hard days. This is your chance to revisit memories and give them shape. If regret lingers, about missed signs, tense moments, or the way things ended, it belongs here too. Name it gently: "I'm sorry for the nights I was too tired to play," or "I wish I could have given you more time outside." The letter becomes a safe container for every feeling, soft and unfiltered.

To help get started, prompts can loosen up words that might otherwise stick in your throat. Try beginning with simple sentences: "My favorite meowmory with you is…" or "It always made me smile when you…" If there's something left unsaid, let it out: "I'm sorry that…" or "If I could go back and change one thing, it would be…" Allow yourself to imagine their side of things, too. "If you could talk back, I imagine you'd say…" Sometimes this exercise brings comfort, picturing your cat's voice, reassuring you or reminding you of the love between you.

Once your letter is finished, think about how to make this ritual tangible. You might tuck the paper into an envelope and place it with your cat's ashes or beside their photo. Some people read their letter aloud during a private farewell ceremony, in a favorite corner of the house or outdoors in a spot their cat loved. Others bury the letter under a new plant or tree, letting nature hold their words as roots grow deep. You could even copy your words into a journal you keep just for "meowmories," adding to it over time as new memories arise or anniversaries come around.

For those who find comfort in sharing, letters can be read with family or friends who also loved your cat. Some choose to write group letters, with each person adding a line or memory, a small chorus of voices sending love across whatever distance remains. If speaking the words aloud feels overwhelming, reading silently in a quiet room beneath soft light can offer its own kind of peace.

These letters aren't only for long-lived companions. Grief after a sudden loss, or for kittens who didn't live many years, matters just as much. One excerpt from a goodbye letter (shared with permission) reads: "Tiny Bit, I never thought our time would be so short. The house feels empty without your wild energy and quick paws chasing shadows on the wall. I wish I could have kept you safe longer." Another, from someone saying goodbye to a mischievous adult cat: "Oliver, you never let me sleep past sunrise and somehow convinced me that every cardboard box was yours by birthright. Thank you for teaching me patience and laughter."

The ritual of letter writing doesn't erase pain, but it gives it form, a place to land outside your mind. It can be revisited whenever the ache resurfaces. Years down the line, reading your own words may bring tears or laughter, or sometimes both in quick succession. Above all, this practice ensures that nothing is left unsaid between you and your cat. The goodbyes become softer when spoken from the heart; they become a bridge between loss and remembrance.

Creating a Memory Garden or Special Space at Home

When the heart aches, and the house echoes with quiet, the urge to create something lasting for your cat's memory comes naturally. For many, the idea of a memory garden or a special spot at home feels like a gentle way to keep love in motion. Picking the right place takes some thought, but you don't need an acre or a green thumb. Sometimes it's just a sunlit windowsill, a cosy nook, or that patch of yard where your cat loved to nap beneath the bushes. Start by noticing where you feel closest to your cat, maybe it's the living room corner that catches every afternoon ray, or a patch outdoors where you both linger on warm evenings. Once you choose your spot, gather a few things that remind you of your cat: a favorite toy, their collar, a small framed photo, or even a note with their name written in your handwriting.

Personalising the space is where healing often starts to bloom. Think about details that capture your cat's true spirit. Did they have a favorite color? Maybe add blue flowers or garden stones in that shade. If your cat adored birdwatching, hang a feeder nearby so the space stays lively. For every year together, you might hang a wind chime, each gentle ring acting as a reminder of another season shared. Plants offer living tribute: choose flowers that come back each year, like daffodils or tulips, or plant a small tree whose branches will stretch upward with time. Some people place a bench nearby to invite quiet reflection. Others dedicate a shelf indoors with keepsakes, a paw print in clay, their name painted on a tile, maybe even an old ID tag nestled among tiny candles.

Tending this space can become its own form of therapy. There's something quietly powerful about watering plants, pulling weeds, or touching smooth stones that bear your cat's name. These small rituals help anchor you in the present while honouring what was lost. You might find yourself talking aloud as you water or sitting quietly among blooming flowers, letting memories drift through the air. On days when sadness feels heavy, tending the garden gives you purpose; each act of care becomes a silent conversation with the one you miss.

This isn't just for adults; kids and family members can find real comfort creating together. Invite children to join by painting stones with little paw prints or writing short messages about their favorite cat memories. A "Meowmories" stepping stone path can wind through the garden, each stone painted with a snapshot of life—"the day she caught her first bug," "the time he climbed the curtains," "her favorite napping spot." Even small hands can plant seeds or arrange tiny figurines in the grass. These rituals help little ones feel included and offer them a language for their own feelings.

Sometimes families create a timeline in the garden, adding one marker for every year spent with their cat, a row of beads strung along a branch, colored ribbons fluttering from a fence, or even simple painted sticks pressed into the soil. Light can play its part too: solar lanterns or fairy lights wound through branches turn evening visits into moments of quiet magic. Indoors, you might clear space on a shelf for objects that hold meaning, a bell from your cat's collar, an old toy mouse, and photos tucked into colorful frames.

Ritual deepens the healing. Consider setting aside time each week to visit this spot, especially on tough days—anniversaries, birthdays, or just when grief bites more sharply than usual. Bring something new: a fresh flower, a note, even just yourself and your thoughts. The act of returning again and again reinforces love's presence and shows your heart that remembrance doesn't have to be all pain; it can include beauty and growth, too.

If you want to include neighbors or friends who also loved your cat, invite them to add something, a poem, a painted stone, or simply their company for a cup of tea by the garden. This turns the memorial into shared ground, filled with stories and laughter as well as tears.

You don't need perfection or grand gestures for this to matter. Sometimes all it takes is one sunflower planted in the earth your cat once padded across, or a tiny altar on your windowsill holding their photo and a tealight candle flickering after dark. Each addition becomes another stitch in the tapestry of memory, living proof that love can root itself in soil and sunlight as surely as it did in fur and purrs.

If you're not sure where to start, stand in the quietest spot of your home or yard and listen for where you feel that familiar tug of memory. That's usually where your tribute will mean the most.

The Power of the Final Catnap & Navigating End-of-Life Choices

Some words hold more comfort than others. Saying "final catnap" instead of death or euthanasia can offer a gentle way to talk about your cat's last moments with children, and we will discuss that further in Chapter 6.

End-of-life care is never one-size-fits-all. Some people want their cats to pass at home, surrounded by familiar scents and gentle voices. Home hospice care allows you to keep routines soft, offering treats, brushing fur, and letting sunlight warm their favorite spot. A compassionate vet can visit and provide comfort-focused medicine and support for both you and your cat. This approach is about making each day count, giving extra tuna, letting them nap wherever they please, and filling the air with calm music or soft words. Others choose a natural passing, keeping their cat comfortable with pain relief, favorite foods, and plenty of affection until nature takes its course. For some families, a ceremonial goodbye is important: planning a "last day" can mean offering every favorite activity, sunbeam naps, special snacks, maybe even a car ride if your cat loved it. You might lay out their beloved blanket in a quiet room and dim the lights, inviting everyone to say what your cat meant to them. There's no official script for these moments, just the intention to surround your cat with love.

The burden of these decisions is heavy. It can feel like you are carrying your cat's entire world on your shoulders, wondering if each step is right.

There's no single correct choice; every option comes with its own mix of sorrow and relief. Some find peace in letting go before suffering begins. Others need every possible day together. The truth is that love underpins every decision, even when it's messy or uncertain. If you're struggling to decide what comes next, try asking yourself what would bring your cat the most comfort or joy in these final days. Sometimes just sitting quietly together or hand-feeding their favorite treat feels like enough.

No matter which path you take, euthanasia with a trusted vet, hospice at home, or a natural goodbye, each is a valid expression of love. The important thing is that you are showing up for your cat with compassion, even when your heart aches with uncertainty. There will always be second-guessing; that's part of caring so much. But trust that the choices made with kindness at their core are never wrong.

Scripts for this stage don't have to be complicated. Honest words serve best: "She's very tired now and needs to rest," or "He's getting ready for his long sleep." If you feel lost for words, lean into presence rather than speech, hold your cat close, let silence speak where words fail. Giving yourself (and others) space to grieve without guilt is one of the most loving things you can do.

Allow yourself to forgive yourself for not having all the answers. Allow yourself tears and relief in the same breath. The act of shepherding your cat through this final transition, however it looks, is an act of devotion that honours every head bump, every purr, every silent moment spent together in the quiet glow of love.

Including Family and Friends: Making Farewells Collaborative

Sometimes, the ache of saying goodbye to your cat feels magnified by the silence in your home. Grieving alone can make even the bravest heart feel fragile, especially when it seems like nobody else truly understands the rawness of your loss. This is where letting others in, whether they're family, friends, or anyone who shared a bond with your cat, can soften that loneliness. Mourning together doesn't erase pain, but it transforms it into something shared, a mosaic of stories and laughter and tears that honours your cat's place in many lives. When you invite people who knew your cat to join you in remembering, you create a circle of comfort and recognition that can make the hardest moments feel less isolating.

Bringing others into your farewell can take many shapes. One gentle approach is to host a small gathering, maybe in your living room, garden, or even virtually if distance separates you, where friends and family are encouraged to share their own memories or funny stories about your cat. It's powerful to hear someone else recall the way your tabby expertly opened kitchen cabinets or the time she photobombed every Zoom call. These shared recollections often spark laughter and tears in equal measure, helping everyone present to process their grief openly. For those who prefer hands-on activities, consider suggesting a group project, such as assembling a scrapbook. Ask each person to contribute a photo or jot down a favorite "meowmory," and assemble these into a colorful collage of moments, paws in the flowerpot, mischief on the windowsill, or quiet cuddles at movie night. Over time, this book becomes a treasure, something you can turn to when you need to feel connected.

A candlelighting ceremony in the garden or on a patio can provide a visual and emotional anchor for collective mourning. Hand out small tea lights or candles to each participant and invite them to light their flame in honour of your cat. As each person says a word or two, or simply stands quietly, you may notice how the soft glow reminds everyone present that love hasn't vanished; it just looks different now. Sometimes people bring poetry, music, or even food that reminds them of your feline companion. These simple acts, woven together, let grief become communal rather than solitary.

It's also important to recognise that not everyone grieves in the same way or on the same timeline. Some family members might be eager to reminisce, while others avoid memories because it feels too raw. Friends could freeze up or withdraw, unsure how to offer comfort. Children might express sadness through artwork or play instead of words. These differences can lead to misunderstandings or even tension if not acknowledged up front. If someone declines to participate or seems distant, try not to take it personally. Everyone processes loss according to their own needs and background. If conversation becomes awkward or emotions flare unexpectedly, remind yourself that these are natural responses; sadness and love often get tangled together.

To make collaborative farewells gentle for everyone involved, set clear expectations and give people permission to grieve in whatever way suits them best. When reaching out, use language that feels open yet non-demanding: "I'd love for you to join us if you feel comfortable, but I understand if you prefer to remember her in your own way." This signals respect for personal boundaries and lets people off the hook if participation would be too much. For group activities like creating a scrapbook or holding a ceremony, offer options: "If you want to write something but aren't ready to share aloud, you're welcome to add it privately later." You might text or call friends with an open invitation: "We're gathering Sunday afternoon to remember Luna. No pressure to speak, just come if you want to be with others who loved her."

If someone expresses worry about "saying the wrong thing," reassure them there's no script for this kind of farewell. Simply being present is enough. For those who find group events overwhelming, suggest smaller rituals, dropping off a card with a memory, sending a photo for your scrapbook, or lighting their own candle at home at the same time as your gathering.

There's no single blueprint for shared mourning, but making space for others can multiply comfort while honouring the many ways your cat touched different lives. Even when stories overlap or memories contradict each other, each voice adds another layer of meaning to your cat's legacy. And when words falter, as they sometimes do, a simple squeeze of the hand or shared silence can speak volumes. Allowing others in, even just a little, can help transform private sorrow into something softer, held together by community and remembrance rather than by loneliness alone.

"Did I Make the Right Call?" & Finding Peace with Your Decisions

AFTER SAYING GOODBYE TO YOUR CAT, IT'S COMMON TO BE HAUNTED by the question, "Did I make the right call?" This doubt creeps in late at night, during moments of quiet, or while sorting through old photos. You might find your mind replaying every choice, every conversation with the vet, and every sign your cat showed in those last days. It's almost universal to wonder if things could have ended differently. You are not alone in this. Everyone who has loved a cat enough to make difficult decisions knows this gnawing uncertainty. Sometimes, replaying events is your heart's way of searching for reassurance or closure; other times, it's simply your love refusing to let go without a fight.

Experts who walk this path with pet owners every day, veterinarians and grief counsellors, have seen these doubts over and over. They often share that the vast majority of decisions around a cat's end-of-life care are made from a place of deep compassion, not neglect or indifference. One veterinarian shared with me, "Quality of life always has to come before quantity. We can only do so much before medical intervention stops being kindness and starts being prolonging suffering." Another counsellor I spoke with explained that guilt after loss is more a reflection of love than of actual mistakes. The simple truth is that medicine has limits. Not every condition can be reversed, no matter how advanced our technology or how much we wish for a miracle. At some point, even the best care cannot turn back time or erase disease.

It helps to step back and honestly assess your intentions during those final weeks or days. Ask yourself: Was I thinking first of my cat's comfort? Did I pay attention to her signals, her appetite, her energy, her ability to enjoy favorite things? Was my decision grounded in love, even if it hurt me deeply? These are not easy questions, but they reveal the heart behind every choice. Imagine if a friend told you the same story; you'd likely see their care and worry, not their faults. Try viewing your own actions with this same gentle lens.

You might also reflect on other questions, such as: Did I seek advice when I felt lost? Did I listen when my cat seemed tired or withdrawn? Did I make space for her needs, even if it meant letting go sooner than I wanted? Often, when we look at our behaviour with honesty and compassion, we see that regret doesn't equate to wrongdoing; it simply means we cared enough to wish for more time.

Moving toward forgiveness is an act of self-respect as much as it is a form of healing. Consider creating a small ritual to help release guilt and accept the past. One approach is to write a personal mantra and post it somewhere you'll see every day. It could be as simple as, "I did my best with what I knew at the time." Light a candle in honour of your cat, and as you watch the flame flicker, imagine your regret rising with the smoke and drifting away. Speak your mantra aloud, letting its truth settle inside you. Over time, repeating this affirmation can help soften the sharp edges of self-judgment.

Some people find comfort in using physical gestures as symbols of letting go, a gentle stroke on a favorite blanket, a small stone released into a river, or even just closing a treasured photo album and whispering, "Thank you. I forgive myself." These acts are not magic, but they give your mind permission to turn toward healing instead of looping through what-ifs.

If regret returns, and it might, remember that you're not expected to become an expert overnight. Loving a cat means facing impossible choices without all the information you wish you had. No one can predict every outcome or anticipate every need. Your cat knew your voice, your touch, your care; those things mattered far more than any decision made in confusion or sadness.

When your heart aches with doubt, pause to remember that second-guessing is simply part of grieving deeply. You acted out of love, and that is what counts most. If you need more support, reach out to someone who understands, a trusted friend, a counsellor, or another cat lover who has walked this road. Sometimes just voicing your worries out loud is enough to lighten their weight.

As this chapter closes, keep in mind that finding peace doesn't mean erasing doubt entirely; it means accepting that love guided you through every hard call. No one's path is perfect or free from regret. What matters is continuing to honour the bond you shared by being gentle with yourself now. In the next chapter, we'll explore how daily reminders can serve as stepping stones toward healing rather than anchors holding you back.

Chapter 4

FACING THE EMPTY WINDOWSILL & RECLAIMING SHARED SPACES

THE DAY AFTER YOU LOSE YOUR CAT, IT'S OFTEN NOT THE BIG, dramatic moments that break you. It's the hush where life used to hum, a patch of sunlight left untouched, a familiar dent in a cushion on the windowsill, the unclaimed spot on your bed that seems to echo with the memory of soft paws. You find yourself pausing at the threshold of a room, eyes fixed on the empty ledge where your cat stretched out to catch the morning rays. Maybe you run your hand over the cushion, feeling for the warmth that used to be there, and all you find is cold fabric and an ache in your chest. These "cat spaces" aren't just furniture, they're living scraps of memory. The armchair where your tabby kneaded before curling up, the laundry basket that inexplicably became a throne, even that one windowsill with a permanent impression from years of feline sunbathing, they're all loaded with meaning. Every time you pass by, you're reminded of a presence that shaped your home in ways friends might never notice.

Sorrow can hit like a tidal wave when you face these spaces. It's easy to avoid them, to keep your distance from the bed's edge or skip sitting in the sunny corner altogether. But often, avoidance just makes the loss bigger, like a shadow spreading across your whole day. Grief isn't something you can sidestep forever. Reclaiming these spaces, gradually and with care, can help you find peace while still honouring what was lost. Start by giving yourself permission to simply be near these spots without expectation. Take your favorite mug and sit for a while in your cat's chosen window seat. Breathe deeply, let your gaze wander, and notice what comes up—there's no right or wrong way to feel here. If tears come, let them fall. If all you can manage is a few minutes before moving away, that's enough for now.

Once sitting there feels less raw, try introducing gentle rituals that connect you to memory and healing at the same time. Bring a notebook or journal and scribble down whatever surfaces, memories, questions, or even small details like how the dust motes look in the morning light. You might write a note to your cat or jot down gratitude for all the ordinary mornings spent together in that very spot. If writing isn't your thing, bring a book and read aloud as if sharing words with your absent companion. Let that space become a place for reflection instead of just hurt.

You don't need to erase their presence to reclaim comfort. Instead, find ways to weave their memory into these corners of your home. Place a framed photo on the windowsill or tuck a small plant into the indentation left by their favorite cushion. Some people find solace in adding a "Whisker Memories" keepsake, a tiny jar holding a whisker found after cleaning, or a small bell from their collar nestled beside a candle. A friend of mine transformed her cat's favorite window perch into her own reading nook. She started each day in that spot with a cup of tea and her journal, sometimes reading aloud passages her cat might have liked. Over time, this ritual turned pain into something softer, a daily act of remembrance that also made space for new comfort.

I've heard from others who found creative ways to honour these spaces, too. One person placed a pot of catnip on the windowsill, letting it grow wild in honour of her mischievous tabby, who never met a plant he didn't sample. Another turned an armchair into a memory seat by draping it with her cat's blanket and adding a plush pillow embroidered with his name. These small acts don't erase longing, but they anchor it, turning loss into legacy.

Reflection Exercise: Reimagining Shared Spaces

Bring a cup of tea or coffee to your cat's favorite spot, maybe the windowsill or that old chair by the radiator. Sit quietly for five minutes and notice which thoughts or emotions arise. Do you feel sadness, gratitude, or irritation at the emptiness? Write down three words that capture what you're experiencing right now. Next, look around: What could you add to this space to make it feel more comforting or meaningful? Maybe it's a photo, maybe it's a plant, or maybe it's just your continued presence there each morning. If you want, sketch out how you'd like this space to look as both a memorial and comfort zone, a place where love and healing can coexist.

You might be surprised how much gentleness grows from these simple rituals, and how gradually these "cat spaces" can start to feel less like wounds and more like places where love lingers—a quiet testament to everything you shared and all you continue to hold close.

What to Do with Cat Toys, Bowls, and Blankets: Letting Go or Holding On?

THERE'S ALWAYS THAT MOMENT YOU OPEN THE CLOSET OR REACH under the couch, and your fingers brush against a fuzzy mouse or a crumpled ball, the kind that used to send your cat into wild, joyful chaos. Maybe you find a battered blanket, worn thin by years of kneading, or a bowl still sporting a faint ring of dried tuna. Each item feels like a tiny museum piece from another life. Deciding what to do with these things stirs up a storm of feelings. Should you keep them? Pass them along? Tuck them out of sight? There's no single right answer. The truth is, your struggle is normal. Some people need to gather all their toys into a box and hide them away for months. Others want to touch and sort each belonging, crying as they remember every quirk and habit. You might even change your mind from day to day, one morning feeling ready to give away a scratching post, the next scooping it up and holding it close. Every approach is valid.

As the days pass, grief often finds its way into the physical spaces your cat once filled. Sorting through your cat's belongings can be surprisingly emotional. These aren't just objects; they're pieces of shared history. If it feels overwhelming, pause. There's no deadline for this work. You can start by gathering everything into a safe spot, such as a basket, a drawer, or even a corner of the room, where you can come back to as you wish. Take each item in hand and notice which memories or emotions rise to the surface. Is this toy linked to a specific story? Does the blanket still carry the faint scent of your cat? Maybe the food bowl reminds you of sleepy mornings side by side in the kitchen. Allow yourself to feel whatever comes: laughter, sadness, or even frustration at how hard this is.

Once you're ready, try gently sorting items into three piles: "keep," "donate," and "memorial." The "keep" pile is for things too precious to part with, maybe their collar, the favorite stuffed animal, or that threadbare blanket. "Donate" is for items in good condition that could bring comfort or fun to another cat in need. If letting go feels impossible right now, it's perfectly fine to box everything up and revisit later. The "memorial" pile is for objects you'd like to transform into something new. If you find the decision paralysing, step away and remind yourself: "It's okay to set this aside and try another day again." There's no rush.

Repurposing cherished items can help shift sorrow into something softer. That ratty blanket might become part of a patchwork quilt or a small pillow, a tactile reminder you can hug on hard days. Some people stitch together scraps from old toys or blankets into a little wall hanging, adding buttons from collars as accents. A shadow box is another beautiful way to gather keepsakes: arrange your cat's collar, a bell, maybe a favourite toy, and a photo or two inside the frame. Hang it somewhere visible so memory feels close but not overwhelming.

If you have an outdoor space or a memory garden, consider weaving in some objects there. A brightly colored toy can nestle among flowers or under a bush your cat used to explore, offering a pop of joy each time you visit. Some folks paint a rock with their cat's name and place it beside an old ball or bell in the garden, a small ritual that keeps memory alive in growing things.

Many struggle with guilt around giving away pet items, fearing it means forgetting. In reality, honouring your own needs comes first. If it soothes you to keep everything for now, that's enough. If passing toys or blankets on to another animal brings comfort, imagine your cat's legacy stretching further, a gentle ripple of kindness reaching out into the world. You might write a note and tuck it with donations: "These belonged to a very loved friend." For some, this act transforms loss into something generous.

When emotions swell unexpectedly, maybe you burst into tears holding a battered mouse toy or feel angry for even having to make these choices, pause and breathe. Repeat softly: "I'm allowed to move at my own speed." If tears come, let them; if numbness arrives instead, trust it will pass. Some days you'll feel strong enough to tackle sorting; other days you'll want to close the drawer and walk away. Both are okay.

If support helps, reach out before you start, maybe ask a friend to join you in sorting through things, or text someone who understands what these objects meant. Sometimes just naming what's hard out loud ("It hurts to see her bowl sitting empty") takes away some of its power. You don't have to face these moments alone.

Above all, remember that there is no expiration date on grief or on love. Whether you turn every toy into a keepsake or give them away in one brave sweep, your choices are yours alone. Every step is its own kind of tribute.

Repurposing the Food Bowl—A Ritual for Reclaiming Routine

Of all the objects left behind, the food bowl might be the one that catches you off guard the most. It sits there, silent and empty, a stubborn witness to every morning and evening spent together. Maybe your hand still reaches for it before your mind can remind you there's no hungry face waiting. The sight of it can be almost unbearable, loaded with longing and a sense of unfinished business. Yet, there's something quietly powerful about this very ordinary object. It carried out daily acts of care, scooping kibble, adding a splash of water, maybe sneaking in some treats on a hard day. Turning that ritual into a new act of healing can help you rewrite the story this bowl tells.

Sometimes, the first step is just to pick it up. Hold it in your hands and really look at it, not just as a leftover, but as a vessel that once delivered comfort and nourishment. If you're ready, fill the sink with warm, soapy water and give the bowl a thorough cleaning. This isn't just about removing stray crumbs; it's about creating a clean slate, a way to honour what was while making space for something new. Let your mind wander as you scrub, remembering the sound of excited paws or the insistent meows that always came before mealtime. Rinse away the suds along with some of the ache.

Now, consider what this bowl might become. Instead of tucking it out of sight or tossing it in a box, invite it back into your life with intention. One idea is to place a small pot of flowers or a succulent inside, a plant that thrives with just a bit of light and water, just like your cat did. Watching green leaves stretch toward the sun can bring a soft kind of hope where pain used to sit. If plants aren't your thing, maybe fill the bowl with smooth stones or marbles, each one representing a cherished memory or a funny story. Over time, you might find yourself adding new stones as memories resurface.

If you want to take the ritual outdoors, consider transforming the bowl into a bird feeder for your balcony or garden. Watching new life gather around something that once belonged to your cat can be surprisingly comforting. It's a way of letting their presence ripple out into the world instead of staying boxed up inside. Some people tuck affirmation cards or folded "meowmory" slips into the bowl, short notes filled with gratitude, silly anecdotes, or even apologies for those days when patience ran thin. On tough mornings, draw a card and read it aloud to start your day with connection rather than emptiness.

For those who prefer something tactile, use the bowl as a catch-all for tiny keepsakes, a bell from an old collar, a favorite button, or even pebbles collected on grief walks. You might place it on your desk or nightstand, where it can hold small reminders of love that are easy to reach for when you need comfort most.

Journaling Prompt: The Bowl's Story

Sit down with pen and paper or open a note on your phone. Write about what this bowl meant in your daily routine, describe feeding times, little quirks (did your cat always nudge it across the floor?), and the feelings attached to those moments. How does it feel to see the bowl now? What does its new role mean to you? Allow yourself to write honestly, whether your words come out as sentences, lists, or just fragments of thought.

Repurposing this object doesn't erase grief, but it nudges you toward healing by turning an everyday ache into an ongoing celebration of care. The bowl changes roles; it continues to hold what matters, just in a different form. Each time you water a plant, fill it with birdseed, or dig through affirmation notes, you're weaving new meaning from old routines.

There's no single right way to do this, only what feels gentle and true for where you are right now. If all you want is to clean it and set it aside for another time, that's enough, too. Your connection to your cat endures in every ritual you choose to create or release.

Handling Anniversaries, Birthdays, and Special Dates

Nothing tugs at your heart quite like those first anniversaries and birthdays after your cat is gone. It's as if the calendar itself turns into a countdown, inching closer to a date you wish you could skip. You sense the heaviness days before it even arrives. The air feels different. Grief sharpens at the edges, as if time is reminding you of all you're missing, one more sunrise curled up together, another year that should have been marked with a silly treat or a new toy. Even ordinary dates become charged with meaning: the day you adopted your cat, the first time they climbed into your lap, or the last time you celebrated a birthday with them sprawled across your presents. The dread leading up to these "firsts" is real, and longing hits with a force that can catch you off guard. If you find yourself counting down, feeling anxious or easily triggered, know this is a normal part of loving deeply.

When these special days arrive, there's no need to pretend you're fine or push away the ache. Instead, consider shaping the day to honour both your grief and your love. Rituals can help. You might bake something sweet, maybe a favorite treat your cat always tried to steal from your plate, and share it with friends or family who understand what this day means to you. Lighting a candle in the evening, especially at the time your cat usually curled up for bed, can create a quiet pause for reflection and connection. The soft flame flickers in the darkness as you remember their warmth and presence. Some people create digital photo montages, scrolling through old pictures, picking out the silliest expressions or the cosiest naps, then sharing them online with others who get it. Posting memories, or even just a single favorite photo, can spark gentle support from friends far and wide; the simple act of sharing keeps the memory alive.

You don't have to mark these dates alone unless that feels best for you. If the company sounds comforting, invite a close friend for a remembrance walk in the park or ask someone over for coffee and stories about your cat. Sometimes just having another person listen as you talk through what this day means is enough to ease the burden. If you're not sure how to ask for support, try saying, "This week will be tough, I'd love some company if you're free," or "Would you mind spending a little time with me on her birthday? It helps to remember her together." For those who prefer solitude, honour that too. There's nothing wrong with closing the door, lighting a candle, and letting memories wash over you in private.

Planning ahead can make these days less overwhelming. Give yourself extra room for self-care, take a day off work if you can, or schedule fewer obligations so you have space to feel whatever surfaces. Some people book a therapy session near anniversaries for added support, while others make sure to stock up on comfort food and cosy blankets. Don't be shy about asking for help or letting others know your needs might change hour by hour. The more kindness you show yourself around these dates, the softer your grief can become.

Special dates also offer unique opportunities for cat-centric rituals. You might write a letter to your cat each year on their adoption day, tucking it into a box with old photos or favorite toys. Others donate supplies to an animal shelter in their cat's name or sponsor a shelter cat who reminds them of their old friend, a living tribute that ripples outward into kindness. You could even plant something new in their memory: a small herb pot on the kitchen windowsill or wildflowers in the yard, watching them grow each year.

The key is not perfection but sincerity; do what feels right for you, even if that changes from year to year. If you wake up on an anniversary and realize all plans feel too heavy, let yourself off the hook and choose rest instead. Sometimes honouring love means simply surviving the hard days with gentleness.

Remember, no date on the calendar can erase what your cat meant to you or dictate how you should feel now. Anniversaries will always carry weight, but they can also be chances to hold memory close and invite healing alongside longing. Whether your ritual is public or private, elaborate or simple, it's yours, and every act of remembrance is another thread tying your heart to theirs, no matter how much time has passed.

Comfort in the Ordinary & Finding New Meaning in Daily Rituals

AFTER LOSING YOUR CAT, THE ORDINARY CAN FEEL LIKE A MINEFIELD. Your morning coffee, for instance, carries echoes of the days when your furry companion padded into the kitchen, tail aloft, demanding breakfast or just company. The quiet that follows now feels unnatural, almost too big for the room. But these daily rituals, so tightly woven with memory, can also become stepping stones back to comfort if you let them evolve instead of vanish.

It might sound simple, but there's power in sitting with your mug in the sunlight and allowing yourself to remember. Sometimes, I find myself tracing patterns in the steam, recalling how my own cat would leap onto the table and press her nose against the window. Instead of shying away from that memory, I let it settle in. I imagine her there, and for a few moments, my coffee becomes a quiet time for gratitude. Perhaps you notice similar moments, maybe while brushing your teeth or folding laundry. You catch yourself expecting a flash of fur, a gentle nudge at your ankle.

Leaning into those pauses, rather than fighting them, can gradually bring surprising comfort.

With time, you may want to adapt old routines to keep your cat's memory close without making every day ache. If you used to water plants together, maybe your cat supervised from the counter, continue that ritual, but pour a little extra care into a dedicated memory plant. Each morning as you water it, say your cat's name out loud or whisper a small thanks for the years spent together. That little act is a bridge between then and now. Others have found meaning in pouring their first cup of tea into a "cat mug" or placing a favorite photo on the breakfast table. It's not about forcing yourself to move on, but about letting love linger in daily life.

Creating new rituals is another way to patch the holes loss leaves behind. A gratitude jar, where you jot down "meowmories" or happy moments whenever one comes to mind, can be comforting on tough days. If you're feeling especially low, reach in and pull out a note: "The time she snored through the thunderstorm" or "How he always interrupted video calls." It's amazing how these small written reminders can spark laughter or tears in equal measure, but mostly they remind you that joy isn't lost; it just changes shape.

Something as simple as wearing a paw print charm on days when grief feels heavy can also help. It becomes a small anchor, a private signal to yourself that you're still connected, even if your companion isn't physically here anymore. I know several people who tuck charms into pockets before big meetings or wear a pendant on what would have been their cat's birthday. The charm doesn't erase pain, but it does offer comfort and a sense of carrying love forward.

I've heard from readers who found peace by weaving new meaning into their daily routines. One woman told me she started taking her morning walk with her cat's collar in her pocket; she'd tap it gently at every corner as if inviting her cat along for the journey. Another person kept a journal open on her kitchen counter and scribbled quick sketches or short notes about silly cat antics whenever they came to mind. A man who never liked journaling began texting himself memories when they popped up during work, tiny digital keepsakes that helped him through rough afternoons.

Daily rituals hold immense potential for healing if we allow them to shift and stretch to fit our new reality. Whether you're stirring cream into coffee while thinking of soft paws or adding water to a thriving green plant that now stands in for your attentive supervisor, you invite memory to blend with comfort. These moments build a patchwork of resilience, a way of saying yes, loss is real, but so is love and so is hope.

As this chapter draws to a close, remember that healing doesn't mean forgetting, and comfort can grow right alongside sadness. Finding new meaning in daily life is an act of courage, a way to honour what was while making space for what comes next. In the following chapter, we'll explore how family and community can help lighten your grief and offer new ways to support both yourself and others through loss.

Chapter 5

THE NINE LIVES TIMELINE: DOCUMENTING YOUR CAT'S MILESTONES

THERE'S A CERTAIN KIND OF MAGIC IN TRACING A CAT'S STORY from beginning to end, a magic that can make your love feel visible, tangible, even when your house is quiet, and paws no longer pad down the hallway. Sometimes, the best way to honour your cat is to see their whole adventure laid out before you, like flipping through a favorite novel where every chapter is filled with mischief, comfort, and the ordinary miracles of daily life. That's where the "Nine Lives Timeline" comes in: it's a tribute that turns memories into something you can touch, see, and revisit anytime. Instead of letting all those moments blur together, you can give each one its own special spot. This isn't just for the dramatic milestones; it's for the small victories, the goofy failures, and the countless firsts that made your cat one of a kind.

To start building your timeline, grab a long piece of ribbon, yarn, or even an old roll of brown paper, the kind that crinkles and feels honest under your fingertips. Lay it out across a table or along a wall. This will be your cat's "life path." Now, think about the moments that truly shaped your relationship. The day you brought them home, maybe they hid under the couch or immediately claimed the sunniest windowsill as their throne. That first purr, hesitant at first but quickly growing into a rumbling declaration of trust. Jot down the silly things too: the time they got stuck in a paper bag or the first time they knocked over your water glass and looked at you like it was your fault. Don't skip over hard memories.

Include the day of their first vet visit, or how they bravely handled moving to a new house. This timeline isn't just about perfection; it's about every messy, beautiful step you took together.

For each "life", each distinct phase or chapter, choose a symbol or color that feels right. Maybe you attach a tiny bell for their kitten years, representing those wild midnight races through the hallway. Use a different color marker or ribbon for adolescence, when their personality really started to bloom, cheeky glances, wild leaps onto countertops, or learning how to open cupboard doors with shocking skill. For mature years, maybe you add a paw print sticker or a pressed flower from their favorite garden spot. If you want to mark a tough phase (an illness or big change), consider tying on a small charm, bead, or even a button from an old shirt they loved to snuggle on.

As you map out each milestone, write a single sentence or word that captures what made it memorable: "First sunny nap," "Met new puppy," "Survived thunderstorm," "Discovered catnip," "Mastered lap-warming." Let the timeline flow naturally, don't worry about making it perfect. Your cat's story probably wasn't neat or linear either. If you're more visual, print out tiny photos and tape them along the line; if you're crafty, draw doodles or use colored pens to highlight transitions between "lives." Some people even hang their timeline on a wall as an art piece, using clothespins to hold photos and notes at each stage.

You can take this digital tribute if that suits you better. There are apps and websites that let you create visual timelines with text and emojis for every event. Maybe you upload your favorite photo for each "life" and add a caption: "First day home," "Sunbeam champion," "Sock thief era." You might even share this timeline with friends online or keep it private as a personal treasure.

I've seen timelines that were simple, a piece of yarn with handwritten cards clipped in order, and others that were elaborate works of art, complete with tiny bells for every "life" and dried catnip leaves pressed at the years' turning points. One reader told me she used colored twine and beads to represent every move her cat made with her, ending with a velvet ribbon tied at the final days as a gentle goodbye. Another person went digital, creating an animated slideshow where each slide was a different emoji-studded "chapter"—from ("kitten chaos") to ("garden explorer") to ("pillow king"). The beauty is in how personal this project becomes; it's yours alone.

Reflection Section: Mapping Your Cat's Nine Lives

Take ten minutes now, grab any scrap paper, open your notes app, or sit quietly with your thoughts. List out nine key lives or phases for your cat. They don't all have to be dramatic, think in seasons: "early mornings together," "the year she learned to fetch," "the old age cuddle era." What symbol would you choose for each one? Is there a scent, color, or object that pops into your mind? Let yourself wander through these memories without judgment. Notice which ones tug hardest at your heart; those may be the lives you most want to celebrate on your timeline.

Every time you walk past your completed timeline, whether it drapes across your living room wall or lives quietly in a drawer, you'll see not just loss but all the richness your cat brought to your days. Documenting their nine lives is more than nostalgia; it's proof that every chapter mattered and every quirky milestone is worth holding close.

Crafting a "Meowmories" Scrapbook or Photo Collage

THERE'S A GENTLE MAGIC IN SIFTING THROUGH OLD PHOTOS, searching for the perfect snapshot of your cat asleep in a sunbeam or mid-pounce on a toy mouse. You pause on those images, remembering the weight of their body on your chest or the way their eyes seemed to light up when you entered the room. Sorting through these moments, you start to realize that every photo, scribbled note, and even the blurry selfies hold a sliver of your shared story. Building a "Meowmories" scrapbook or photo collage isn't just about organizing keepsakes; it's about weaving your cat's legacy into something you can hold, revisit, and cherish on the hardest days. There's comfort in the tactile process of touching familiar faces and arranging them in a way that feels true to your bond. You may even find yourself smiling through tears as you spot a forgotten memory: the time your cat squeezed into a shoebox or dozed across a laundry pile, oblivious to the chaos around them.

When you begin this project, it helps to think about themes that reflect your cat's personality and quirks. Rather than arranging everything chronologically, consider dedicating pages or sections to their "firsts"—first day home, first successful leap to the forbidden countertop, first time they met the neighbor's dog. Maybe you want a whole spread celebrating their favorite napping spots, each photo capturing a new discovery: curled up in the bathroom sink, stretched across a sunny windowsill, or nestled inside a crinkly grocery bag. Humor finds its place too; create a "funniest moments" gallery with snapshots of their wild zoomies, derpy yawns, and costume mishaps. Did your cat love holidays? Make a page for each silly hat or festive collar, or assemble all the times they attempted (and sometimes succeeded at) climbing the Christmas tree. For those extra-special bonds, add a section called "catnap companions" featuring photos of you together, on the couch, in bed, or side by side during a lazy afternoon.

The materials you use can transform this from a simple album into a living tribute. Choose paper that feels good in your hands—something thick or textured. Colored pens, markers, and washi tape add visual interest and warmth. Paw print stamps or stickers can march across pages, marking milestones. Ribbons from your cat's favorite toys can be tied onto page edges, creating tactile reminders. Pressed flowers from your garden or from walks you shared together offer a natural touch; glue petals beside photos of garden explorations or window-watching sessions. Handwritten notes bring your voice into the story: scribble anecdotes in the margins ("You always stole my spot, but I loved it") or add date captions beneath each picture. For cats who loved adventure (even if it was just to the kitchen), create a "box adventures" page filled with photos of cardboard conquests and tipsy towers.

If looking at an empty page makes you freeze up, prompts and templates give you momentum. Start with printable collage grids, squares for photos, circles for doodles, and spaces for short sentences. Use journaling prompts to fill in blank spots: "My favorite thing about you was…" "You always made me laugh when…" "The silliest thing you ever did…" Even one sentence beside each image can speak volumes. Consider writing a letter to your cat and tucking it into an envelope pasted inside; sometimes, what you need most is space for unsaid words.

For those who want structure but lack the time or energy to design from scratch, pre-made templates ease the pressure. Many craft stores sell themed scrapbook kits with backgrounds, frames, and stickers that fit pet memories perfectly. You can print simple checklists, "Favorite toys," "Best hiding spots," "Most mischief caused", and fill them in as you go. Some people like to dedicate one page per year, marking big changes with a different border color or sticker style. Others prefer mood-based organization: a "comfort page" for all those calm cuddles, a "wild side" page for every blurry action shot.

You don't need to be an artist to make something beautiful or meaningful. What matters most is that each page feels honest, a reflection of both the joy and sorrow wound through your time together. If you want, invite friends or family to contribute their own notes or pictures;

sometimes others capture moments you never saw. If you're comfortable with technology, try mixing printed photos with digital images. Many online services let you design collages and order them as posters or bound books.

Even if you only finish one page at a time, each step is an act of honouring love and loss alike. There is no wrong way to capture your meowmories; every scribble, pressed flower, sticker paw print, and handwritten story adds another layer to the tapestry of your cat's life, a story worth telling again and again.

DIY Paw Print Keepsakes and Whisker Memory Jars

MAKING A KEEPSAKE BY HAND AFTER LOSING YOUR CAT CAN BE grounding and comforting. Crafting a paw print or saving a whisker isn't about artistic skill, just the willingness to transform feelings into something tangible. These simple projects offer solace and keep your cat's memory alive in a tactile way.

If your cat is still with you, creating a paw print impression can become a gentle farewell ritual. Air-dry clay, commonly found at craft stores, is soft and forgiving. Knead a small ball, then flatten it into a disc or heart about half an inch thick. Gently press your cat's paw onto the surface to make an imprint, avoiding any discomfort. If your cat has passed, many vets offer to take a paw print after euthanasia; don't hesitate to ask. Alternatively, use a non-toxic ink pad to capture the print on sturdy paper or cardstock. For salt dough, simply mix 1 cup of flour, 1/2 cup of salt, and 1/2 cup of water; knead, flatten, and press the paw before baking over low heat. Before the clay hardens or the dough bakes, inscribe your cat's name and the date, perhaps adding a brief message or symbol.

Once dried, your impression can be painted or left natural. Making a small hole at the top lets you string it as an ornament, hang it on a wall, near your desk, or in your car. Others prefer to keep it in a memory box or display it with framed photos. Wherever placed, these keepsakes invite quiet moments of connection and serve as comforting touchstones when grief feels raw.

Whiskers have a near-mystical presence, and finding one after your cat's gone can feel like a message from beyond. Collect whiskers gently, never pluck, only gather those shed naturally. Collect tufts of fur from grooming or bedding, too. Store them in a small glass vial, locket, or jar; apothecary-style bottles work well, but any tiny container you like is suitable.

Personalizing Your Memory Jar

Enhance your keepsake by adding dried lavender, rose petals, or a scrap of ribbon from a favorite toy. Attach a hand-written tag with your cat's name for a personal touch. Place these jars somewhere meaningful: on a shelf among favorite books, near cheerful houseplants, or tucked away in a private drawer with other cherished mementoes.

Handling these keepsakes, feeling their weight or tracing their shape, is grounding and can ease anxiety. They can become part of your daily ritual, offering brief comfort when you pause at them or hold them, especially on anniversaries or hard days.

Display Ideas

Display your keepsakes in ways that suit your routines. Hang a paw print ornament by the front door to welcome you home, or set a whisker jar on your mantel among treasured items. Frame clay impressions with photos from kittenhood to old age to create personal altars of remembrance. Some people tuck them into pockets or bags for everyday reassurance, carrying a tangible reminder wherever they go.

You can also place keepsakes in places where you naturally reach for comfort, such as your nightstand, your workspace, or a coat pocket. These objects don't erase the pain, but they make grief easier to bear by reminding you that love endures in new forms.

Adding Written Memories

To go further, jot down feelings or memories as you create your keepsake, write short notes or messages to slip into the jar. Express what was unique about your bond: "You always knew when I needed company," "Your purrs healed long days," or simply, "You made this house home." Over time, you'll accumulate a small archive of written comfort, layering extra meaning into the keepsake.

Finding Comfort

Making memorials may bring tears at first, but can also spark laughter and relief as you remember happier times. Each time you see or hold your keepsake, let it remind you that the bond with your cat still lingers, a soft curve of clay, a whisker catching the light, or a simple token offering comfort. Love persists, gently changing form but always remaining within reach.

Planting a Living Tribute & Choosing the Right Plant or Tree

There's something deeply comforting about nurturing life in memory of a loved cat. When grief leaves your home feeling still, planting can help keep the connection alive. Watching new leaves unfurl, or a flower bloom where emptiness once lingered, reminds you that love sticks around in small, persistent ways. Living memorials do more than decorate a space; they become ongoing reminders of your cat's spirit, woven into every leaf and petal. Each day, as you water, prune, or simply sit beside your chosen plant, you're participating in an act of gentle healing. It's not just about the end; it's about honouring the entire arc of your cat's life by tending to something that grows and changes just as your relationship did.

Picking the right plant is a personal choice, a chance to match greenery with your cat's distinct personality. Consider your lifestyle first: If you don't have a yard or live in an apartment, don't worry. There are plenty of beautiful indoor options that thrive on windowsills, bookshelves, or even in hanging baskets. A sun-loving succulent might suit a cat who always found the brightest patch of light for an afternoon nap. Their thick, sturdy leaves offer resilience and low-maintenance care, perfect if you're overwhelmed or new to plant keeping. For a playful spirit who never tired of exploring, try catnip or catmint. Both are easy to grow in pots and spill over with energy, almost as if your cat's curiosity found a way to keep romping through your home. If your companion always seemed colorful and full of surprises, a flowering bush like hydrangea or azalea can capture that vibrancy, with bursts of blooms echoing the joy they brought you. Lavender or rosemary, with their calming scents, may work well for cats who soothed your anxious moments with slow blinks and purrs.

Outdoor spaces open up even more options. Dogwood trees, cherry blossoms, or crepe myrtles create gentle beauty and shade, a lovely tribute for cats who loved watching birds from the porch or basking beneath branches. Memorial gardens can be as simple as a single rose bush or as elaborate as a winding path lined with wildflowers. For those living where winters bite hard, evergreens like juniper or holly offer year-round color and resilience. If you're honouring a cat who weathered storms or overcame challenges, consider a tree known for endurance, oak or ginkgo, plants that grow stronger with time.

Once you've chosen your green companion, planning the dedication is where emotion and ritual come together. On planting day, gather whatever feels meaningful: a favorite toy (maybe that battered mouse with half its stuffing gone), a collar bell, or even a pinch of fur you saved from grooming sessions. Dig the hole or prepare the pot with intention; maybe light a nearby candle or play soft music that always seemed to calm you both. Place the memento gently in the soil as you settle the roots; this small act links memory and growth in a way words rarely can. Speaking aloud can help release tangled feelings. You might say, "Thank you for every sunrise and every soft paw at my door," or read a short poem that captures your gratitude and love.

If gathering with others brings comfort, invite friends or family to share stories or help with planting. Children especially like to drop a favorite toy or draw a picture to bury alongside the plant's roots. Afterwards, you can mark the spot with a painted stone or simple marker bearing your cat's name and dates, a quiet declaration that this patch of earth has special meaning.

Caring for your living tribute becomes its own kind of ongoing ritual. Watering isn't just routine; it's a time to check in with your emotions and honour the bond that shaped both you and your cat. Some people set aside time each week to sit by their memorial plant, sharing memories aloud or in a journal as they watch new growth appear. Pruning dead leaves, picking flowers for a vase, or even just tracing the shape of a leaf can ground you when grief flares up unexpectedly. These small acts let you reflect on how life continues, different now, but still beautiful.

Through storms and sunny days alike, tending to something alive helps anchor you when memories threaten to slip away. Even when sadness feels sharpest, seeing fresh shoots pushing through soil can spark gratitude for all the ordinary days you shared, a living tribute that whispers: love never really leaves; it just finds new ways to grow.

Virtual Memorials: Sharing Your Cat's Story Online

Sometimes, when the ache of loss feels too big for one heart to carry, the comfort of community can do wonders. The world has changed in so many ways, and grieving is no exception. Virtual memorials have become a powerful and surprisingly healing tool. They make it possible to gather memories, tributes, and photos in one place, letting your cat's story ripple out beyond the walls of your home. There's something meaningful about seeing loving messages from friends who knew your cat, or even from strangers who simply understand what it means to love and lose a feline companion. In a time when you might crave both connection and privacy, digital spaces let you shape your memorial to fit exactly what you need. The right platform can give you a place to return to whenever you want, a kind of living archive that grows with every shared story.

If you're thinking about creating an online tribute, there's no shortage of options. Some people start with a simple social media post on Facebook or Instagram, sharing favorite photos and a few heartfelt words. Others build dedicated pages using pet memorial sites, which often offer templates for uploading images, stories, and even videos. When choosing where to share, consider where you feel most comfortable and where your friends and family already gather online. A Facebook post can quickly reach those who've met your cat over the years, while a dedicated Instagram Story or highlight reel offers a more visual tribute, perfect for those cats with big personalities and even bigger photo collections. Pet memorial websites let you create something a little more permanent and private, should you prefer a quieter space.

The story you tell can be as simple or detailed as you like. I've found that writing a "life story" post—almost like an obituary but filled with love and quirks, can be incredibly cathartic. Instead of just listing dates, focus on the moments that made your cat irreplaceable. Maybe you write about their obsession with cardboard boxes or the way they always seemed to know when you needed comfort. Pair these words with your favorite photos, sunbeam naps, yawning stretches, goofy costumes, or dignified stares. If your cat had a hashtag or nickname, use it so others can find and contribute to the conversation. For those who love video, string together short clips into a highlight reel; Instagram Stories let you pin these as permanent fixtures on your profile, making them easy to revisit whenever nostalgia strikes.

One of the most beautiful aspects of online memorials is how they invite others to join in. After posting your tribute, consider asking friends and family to add their own memories or photos in the comments. Start a "memory thread" by encouraging people to share their favorite stories, maybe that time your cat crashed a Zoom call or curled up on an unsuspecting guest's lap. If your circle is small, even a handful of messages can make a big difference; if you have a wide community of animal lovers, you might be surprised by how many people want to celebrate your cat's life alongside you. Interaction isn't just about gathering likes or hearts; it's about seeing your grief reflected in others' words, and realizing your companion mattered to more than just you.

Of course, sharing online also means navigating boundaries, both emotional and practical. It's perfectly valid to keep some memories private while sharing others with the world. Before posting, pause to consider what feels right: are there stories or photos that are just for you? Is there anything you'd rather not see discussed publicly? Most platforms let you adjust privacy settings so that only trusted friends can view or comment. On pet memorial websites, you can often moderate posts or approve messages before they go live. If you find yourself overwhelmed by attention or receive comments that sting (and unfortunately, this can happen), don't hesitate to take a step back. Remind yourself that this space is for your healing first and foremost, not for meeting others' expectations.

It's normal to worry about judgment or unkind remarks online, especially when sharing something as vulnerable as grief. If this fear holds you back, start with a small group, maybe just close friends or family, in a private message thread or group chat. You might open the memorial to a wider audience later, when you feel ready. Give yourself permission to delete or ignore any responses that don't feel supportive; protecting your heart is an act of self-respect.

Your virtual memorial doesn't need to be polished or perfect. It just needs to feel honest, to reflect the love, the messiness, the laughter, and the sorrow that made your connection with your cat so unique. Whether it's a short post with a favorite photo or an entire website filled with stories and videos, what matters is that it feels true to you and honours the cat who changed your life. Grief can feel isolating, but digital spaces offer gentle reminders that even in loss, community and compassion are always within reach.

Rituals and Ceremonies: Creating Your Own Goodbye

For many, this need to remember eventually becomes a desire to say goodbye in a more personal way. Saying farewell to your cat deserves more than quiet sadness and a fading memory. There's real healing in pausing, gathering your thoughts, and honouring your loss with a ritual that feels meaningful to you. Rituals, formal or informal, offer structure when your emotions feel scattered, and help transform pain into remembrance. You don't need incense or fancy words; what truly matters is intention. Taking time to mark your cat's passing, in any way that resonates, provides a grounding anchor when grief feels overwhelming.

To create your own ceremony, start by reflecting on what soothed or defined your cat. Did music calm them? Play that song now, letting it fill the space with comfort. If there's a letter, poem, or message you've written or wish you had, read it aloud, perhaps at dusk when the world is quieter. Lighting a candle can symbolize memory and gratitude: each flame a memory, each flicker a tiny thank-you. Sometimes, I speak a memory out loud as I light a candle, things like how my cat chased sunbeams or crawled onto my lap on hard days. Placing a toy in a special spot or scattering their favorite treats in the garden can connect your actions to memory and emotion.

Ceremonies don't have to be elaborate or public. Introverts may find comfort in a private ritual, a quiet walk to a favorite park bench, or sitting in their cat's spot by the window with tea. Those who grieve best in company may wish to include friends or family, even briefly. Children often bring honest emotions and can be part of the ceremony through drawings or letters, which can be read aloud, shared, or buried with a special object under a tree. Involving others can turn solitary sadness into communal support and healing.

Rituals can also be revisited as anniversaries or special occasions return. Marking these moments keeps your cat's memory alive and allows space for recurring feelings. Maybe you bake something sweet on your cat's birthday, fill your home with warmth, and share stories as you eat. Spring could become a time to plant new flowers in a memory garden, each bloom telling part of your cat's story. Lighting a candle on the day your cat died is a simple annual act that says their spirit endures. Some people find comfort in naming a "remembrance day" each year—looking at photos, listening to a song, or sitting quietly to reflect.

Ultimately, the ritual should fit you, not any tradition or outside expectation. If you prefer a private farewell, honour that. If you'd rather gather friends for a sunset toast, that's just as meaningful. There's no script; just be authentic. Small gestures—like tying a ribbon to a branch or placing a stone with your cat's name on it- can be deeply significant.

If you're unsure where to start, jot down three things that remind you of your cat, a favorite sound, scent, or time of day, and build a ritual around those. Each ceremony is as unique as the bond you shared. Don't judge your tears or your laughter; both are natural at a healing ceremony.

As months and years pass, rituals may evolve. You might add new elements or let old ones fall away as your grief changes and happier memories emerge. The goal isn't perfection, but presence, a commitment to honouring your bond, especially when words fail.

Creating space for an intentional goodbye gives your grief a safe outlet. It won't erase the ache, but it will soften it, reminding you not only of the pain of loss but also the love that came before.

Rituals and ceremonies help us find meaning and comfort in loss, allowing us to take action even as we remember. These small acts can become stepping stones toward peace. Next, we'll look at how families, adults and children can find healing together, supporting one another through grief.

Chapter 6

How to Talk to Children About a Cat's Death & Words That Comfort

WHEN A CAT DIES, IT CHANGES THE HOUSEHOLD dynamic. Adults often feel it first, but children take it in, sometimes quietly and other times with difficult questions. It can be hard for adults to know what to say, but children value honesty more than perfect answers. As they grow, their understanding of loss deepens, but their need for safety and love never fades.

Explaining death can seem daunting. While it's tempting to spare children's feelings with softened phrases like "Whiskers went away" or "She's sleeping," vague words can create confusion or fear. Young kids notice their pet's absence and the changes. Gentle honesty is best. Use clear words, such as "She died" or "She took her final catnap." This helps children link their feelings to reality. If your family believes in the Rainbow Bridge, you can offer, "Some people say cats cross the Rainbow Bridge when they die, a peaceful place where they aren't sick or hurting." This blends comfort with truth and gives children a visual for their imagination.

Children grieve differently depending on their age and experience. A preschooler might ask, "When will Whiskers come home?" while an older child could want to know what death means physically or spiritually. If your child asks, "Why did she have to go?" anchor your response in love and facts: "She was very sick, and her body stopped working. We loved her so much, and it wasn't anyone's fault." If a child worries, "Is my cat hurting now?" you can reassure, "No, she doesn't feel pain anymore. She's at peace now." Honest, soothing answers help kids process loss while feeling secure in your support.

Children's questions may arrive suddenly or recur for weeks. Some will want repeated conversations; others will grow quiet and grieve internally. Don't pressure them to mourn in a certain way. Some may draw pictures, leave toys at the cat's favorite spot, or ask if she'll return. You can gently reply, "I wish she could come back, too. I miss her every day." This helps kids feel heard, not dismissed.

Adult grief can be unsettling for kids to witness, but showing sadness demonstrates that it's safe to feel emotions. If you cry, don't hide it; say, "I'm crying because I miss Whiskers. It's okay to be sad when we lose someone we love." This gives permission for feelings like tears, laughter at memories, anger, or confusion. It shows grief doesn't need to be dealt with in silence or alone.

Some children work through loss with play, using stuffed animals, pretend vet games, or imaginary conversations about their cat. These aren't avoidance; they're a child's way of processing on their terms. Respect these expressions by joining if invited, without forcing participation.

Reflection Section: Comfort Scripts for Children's Hardest Questions

Review and adapt these scripts to your family's needs:

- **"Why did she have to go?"** "She was very sick, and her body couldn't get better anymore. We loved her so much and did everything we could."

- **"Is my cat hurting now?"** "No, she isn't hurting now. She feels peaceful."

- **"Will I ever see her again?"** "I don't know for sure, but some people believe we'll see our pets again one day. What do you think?"
- **"Is it okay to feel sad?"** "Yes, it's normal to feel sad when we miss someone special. I feel sad too."
- **"When will I stop missing her?"** "Missing someone can last a long time. The missing part gets easier to carry as time goes on."

Allowing children to grieve in their unique way and responding with gentle honesty not only helps them cope now but also strengthens their ability to face loss with compassion in the future. Your openness sets a healthy example that will support them long after this moment.

Involving Kids in Memorial Projects: Creative Healing as a Family

ONE WAY TO SUPPORT THAT PROCESS IS BY GIVING CHILDREN something tangible to hold onto. When a cat's absence fills your house, one of the most powerful things you can do is to bring your children into the process of remembrance. Kids, even those who seem distracted or unfazed, absorb loss with a depth that adults sometimes overlook. Including them in simple, creative rituals gives them a way to process, honour, and remember alongside you, turning heartbreak into connection. Instead of feeling pushed aside by adult sorrow or confused by silence, they get a role in saying goodbye and holding on.

Sometimes, what helps most isn't talking, it's doing something gentle with those feelings. Hands-on projects are more than busywork; they're a bridge between memory and healing. Decorating a memory box is a classic project that works for almost any age. Give your child a plain box and invite them to cover it with stickers, drawings, or even glued-on bits of their favorite blanket or collar. Let them choose items to tuck inside, a photo, a jingle bell, maybe a small toy the cat used to bat around the kitchen floor.

The box becomes a safe, tangible place for memories that can be opened whenever someone misses their friend. Older kids might want to write notes or stories to slip inside, while younger ones often prefer to just draw the cat's silly sleeping pose or favourite treat.

Another beautiful activity is planting flowers together in a spot that holds meaning for your family. Pick seeds or small plants, sunflowers, catnip, marigolds, anything easy to tend. As you dig and water, talk about what made your cat special. Maybe you could mention how she used to nap in the garden or chase butterflies in the grass. Each bloom becomes a gentle, living tribute. Little hands can help scatter seeds or place painted stones around the base, turning gardening into an act of remembrance.

Family storytelling sessions transform grief into laughter and warmth. Gather everyone in the living room or around the kitchen table; there's no need for a formal occasion. Start by sharing your favorite memory of your cat's quirkiest moment: "Remember when she tried to fit into that shoebox and got stuck?", that sort of thing. Then invite each child to add their own. Maybe one recalls the thunderous "zoomies" through the hallway at 3 am, another remembers the time she knocked over a glass of water just to watch it splash. These stories don't have to be dramatic; even tiny details spark comfort and a sense of belonging. Sometimes children remember things you've forgotten, like how your cat always waited at the door when they came home from school, or their habit of stealing hair ties from bathroom counters.

To keep your cat's memory active and woven into family life, ongoing rituals work wonders. Baking "cat paw" cookies on your cat's birthday is a sweet tradition that grows with your kids. Rolling out dough, pressing in chocolate chips for toes, and sharing stories while you bake. It doesn't matter if the cookies are Pinterest-perfect; what matters is the togetherness and the permission to remember out loud. Some families create a "meowmories" journal kept in a special spot, each person adds to it whenever they like. It could be a quick sketch, a glued-in photo, or just a line about something that made them think of their cat that day.

See if your kids want to revisit these rituals on anniversaries, holidays, or random afternoons when missing feels sharpest. Maybe you light a candle together before dinner once a month or let everyone write down something they miss and read it aloud as a group. Let these rituals shift as your children grow; what feels right now may change in a year or two.

Family Project: The Memory Box Activity

- Gather an empty box (shoeboxes work well) and set out art supplies: markers, stickers, fabric scraps, and glue.

- Invite everyone to decorate their piece of the box however they like; there are no rules.

- Talk about which items feel important to include. Photos? A collar? A yarn ball? Let each child decide for themselves.

- Once everything is inside, choose whether to keep the box in a public spot or let each child have their own.

- Return to the box whenever someone feels sad or happy, and add new memories as they come.

Bringing kids into these acts of remembrance gives them agency and comfort while showing them that grief, though painful, can be softened by creativity and shared love. The projects might seem simple on the surface, but for a child's heart, these small rituals are powerful medicine for loss.

Helping Other Pets Grieve: Recognizing and Easing Their Sadness

When a cat leaves the household, the emptiness can settle not just in the hearts of people but also in the very skin and senses of other pets who shared life under the same roof. You might notice subtle changes right away, or sometimes only after days of quiet. For many pets, the loss of a companion is confusing. They don't have words for grief, but their bodies and routines tell the story. A dog may circle favorite sleeping spots, sniffing for a scent that's fading, or sit at the window waiting for a friend who never returns. Another cat might call out in the night, searching for a familiar answer in the dark, or simply withdraw to a corner, curled tighter than usual. Appetite can shift, sometimes eating less, sometimes begging for treats they once ignored. Sleep patterns go haywire; you could see more pacing at odd hours or lethargy that feels almost like depression. Some pets become clingy, following you from room to room, unwilling to let you out of sight. In contrast, others keep their distance, as if solitude is the only comfort left.

You might find your remaining pets wandering the house with a kind of restlessness, investigating the places their friend used to nap or prowl. Searching behavior is common: sniffing bedding, peering behind furniture, listening at doors for footsteps that will not come. It can pull at your heart to watch, this visible longing in an animal who cannot ask questions or get answers. Sometimes, pets vocalize more, giving out plaintive meows or quiet whimpers that feel like they land more heavily in the silence after loss. If you spot any of these signs, a change in food interest, altered sleep, searching, extra vocalizing, withdrawal, or even accidents in the house, it's likely your pet is working through grief in their own way.

Supporting a grieving pet takes patience and a willingness to adapt routines gently. Stability becomes your ally; try to keep feeding and play schedules steady so your pet knows what to expect each day. The comfort of predictability helps anchor them when so much else has changed. Carve out time for regular walks or play sessions, even if energy feels low on both sides. Sometimes, just tossing a favorite toy down the hallway or dragging a string across the floor can bring a spark of normalcy back. If your remaining cat seems uninterested in typical games, introduce something novel: a crinkly tunnel, a new scratching post, or even a window perch where they can observe birds and squirrels outside. These small enrichments invite curiosity and movement, a helpful antidote to sorrow.

Another way to help is by gently encouraging your pet to explore spaces that belonged to their companion. Place cozy blankets or beds in those spots, adding items with your scent for reassurance. Don't force things; let your pet decide when and if they want to occupy those spaces. Sometimes, simply sitting in those places with your pet nearby can offer comfort without words. If they seem especially lonely, schedule extra cuddle time on the couch or bed. Stroking fur or scratching behind ears can settle anxiety for both of you and strengthen bonds during a season of loss.

You may wonder about introducing new animal friendships as a remedy for loneliness. While it's tempting to fill the empty space with another pet right away, it's wise to give surviving animals time to process before changing the household dynamic again. Some pets do welcome new company quickly; others need weeks or months before they're ready for another bond. Watch their body language. If your pet perks up around other animals on walks or through the window, that's a sign they may be open to new friends. For now, you can increase your own companionship, spending extra time in play, grooming, or even just sharing quiet moments together.

Sometimes grief in pets lingers longer than you expect or seems to get worse with time instead of better. You should watch for changes in appetite that persist for more than a few days, and if your cat's weight drops sharply, or if your cat's sleep is constantly disturbed, or if your cat withdraws from all interaction, these are signs it's time to consult your veterinarian. Medical issues can sometimes masquerade as grief, so it's important not to assume sadness is always the cause. In some cases, a referral to an animal behaviorist is helpful; these professionals can suggest strategies tailored to your cat's unique needs and temperament.

Helping another pet through loss means tuning in without pressuring them to "move on." Grief in animals is as real and variable as it is for people; some bounce back after a few days with extra attention, while others need more time and support. Observe carefully, stay flexible with your care, and don't hesitate to reach out for professional guidance if you sense something deeper at play. Your awareness makes all the difference; every small gesture of comfort you offer meets your surviving pet right where they are.

Grieving Together: Supporting Your Partner or Housemates

Losing a cat affects everyone in the home. The absence can shift moods, disrupt routines, and change how you relate to one another. Each person's grief may become more visible: you might want to talk or reminisce, while your partner becomes quiet and withdrawn. Maybe you find comfort in sharing stories, while a housemate deals with feelings by staying busy. This mismatch can feel isolating, especially when you need each other most.

It's completely normal for adults to grieve in different ways. One person might need to talk about the cat regularly, question decisions, or repeatedly look at photos. Others might say nothing for days, turning to hobbies, work, or walks to cope. Neither approach is better; they are just different styles that can occasionally lead to tension. You might worry someone didn't care as much, or feel alone in your grief. Meanwhile, someone inwardly mourning might feel overwhelmed by repeated conversations.

Gentle conversations can ease some of this strain. You don't need grand speeches, just simple check-ins like, "How are you holding up about

Muffin today?" or "I noticed you seemed quiet after seeing the food bowl, want to talk?" These questions invite conversation without demanding it. If you need something specific, be clear yet kind: "I'd love to share a story about Muffin if you're up for it," or "If you want space tonight, that's okay too." Sometimes, simply acknowledging the grief can soften tensions.

Shared Rituals

Shared rituals can help bridge differences when words don't come easily. These can be simple: lighting a candle together at dinner for a week or pausing together to remember your cat can offer comfort without requiring conversation. Making a shared digital photo album offers a gentle way to share memories; some days you might add a photo, other days you might just scroll together in silence. If you're comfortable, pick a weekly moment, maybe over coffee, to share something you miss or appreciate about your cat.

Rituals might also mean working on a joint project: a memorial shelf, a playlist of songs that remind you of your cat, or cooking her favorite "people food" once more. Even writing her name on a stone and keeping it by the door can serve as a shared gesture. These acts create a connection even when emotional responses differ.

Navigating Different Grief Timelines

Friction can arise when grief timelines don't match. One partner might want another cat soon, craving activity and companionship; the other might need months before considering it, not ready to "replace" their lost friend. These differences aren't about love for the cat but about different coping needs. When disagreement arises, pause before reacting. Try, "I hear that another cat might help you heal. I'm not there yet, but let's talk again in a few weeks," or, "I know you're not ready, but could we at least discuss what adopting again might look like in the future?"

Sometimes silence, not disagreement, causes misunderstanding. A withdrawn partner may simply be coping, not showing a lack of care for you or the cat. Instead of assuming, ask gently what support would help, and reassure them you're there when they want to talk.

Managing Frustrations

Shared grief can magnify minor annoyances; small habits, like the way someone loads the dishwasher, can suddenly feel unbearable. Try not to let minor irritations become battlegrounds for deeper sadness. Remind yourself that everyone is hurting in their own way.

Continuing Support

Most importantly, keep showing up for each other, even imperfectly. You don't have to grieve the same way or agree on every step. What matters is demonstrating that love and support persist despite loss. Sometimes that means silent togetherness, a shared quiet moment on the couch. Other times, it's simple gestures: making tea, leaving a note, or a comforting hug when words aren't enough.

Grieving together is unpredictable and often messy. There will be awkward moments and mismatched needs, but regular check-ins and shared rituals can prevent resentment and remind you that even amid loss, connection remains possible.

Blending Different Grief Styles & Respecting Each Other's Process

In every home, grief takes many forms. Some people need to share memories and talk through their pain, while others keep their sadness private, not because they care less, but because it feels safer or more manageable. One person might find comfort reminiscing with family, while another prefers a private candlelit moment after everyone's asleep. Neither way is wrong. It's easy to question whether you're grieving "correctly" if your approach doesn't match someone else's, but there's no single right way to mourn. One person needing to talk doesn't negate another's need for quiet. If we don't acknowledge these differences, they can easily lead to misunderstandings.

After a loss, family members often tiptoe around each other's feelings or avoid bringing up the pet, worried about making others even sadder. Those who share openly may feel frustrated by silence; those who grieve inwardly might feel overwhelmed by group displays of sadness or affection. Often, these mismatches breed distance when comfort is needed most.

Patience and honest communication help bridge these gaps. If you need space, say so: "I'm not ready to talk about her today, but I like hearing stories when I feel better." If sharing helps, you can say: "Talking about Miso helps me. Are you okay with that?" Such directness sets boundaries while still offering connection. There's no need to force togetherness, but leaving an open invitation for support or stories allows everyone to participate when they're ready.

Creating small, pressure-free rituals is a good compromise. For example, designate a weekly "memory moment" after dinner or during a walk, when anyone can share a memory or simply sit in quiet company. Participation is always optional; people can choose to join, listen, or sit out. Over time, these little traditions can lower walls and encourage trust, reassuring everyone that their feelings matter.

Some families find their own ways to remember together and apart. For instance, a parent might write notes about their lost cat on the porch each night while children make collages or laugh over photos at the kitchen table. Occasionally, these paths cross, a parent joining the children, or watching quietly. With no judgment or pressure, everyone can honour their loss differently, which helps genuine healing and reduces resentment.

When a child wants to join a group remembrance and another family member prefers solitude, respecting these preferences can be hard if you're desperate for togetherness. But forcing someone to join in can backfire. It's better to check in gently: "Would you like to join us? If not, that's okay." Such invitations reassure loved ones they're wanted, without making grief into a duty.

Some families keep a dry-erase board on the fridge for "cat memories," letting anyone add a doodle or note whenever they wish. Others maintain a shared digital album of photos and stories, accessible to everyone at their own pace. These low-pressure options help keep memories alive without singling anyone out.

If left unspoken, differences in grieving can feel like rejection. Remind yourself, and others, that privacy is not indifference. Some people process loss by walking alone or throwing themselves into work, while others fill the house with laughter and stories. Trust grows when everyone acknowledges that all feelings are valid, and no style of missing someone is better than another.

If tempers flare or tears come unexpectedly, hit pause. Try naming what's going on: "I think we're both missing her in our own ways right now." Saying this out loud can soften the tension and bring understanding.

Grief styles may change over time. Someone needing space early on may seek out group rituals later, just as someone who shared openly at first might prefer quiet remembrance later. Allow each other to change without guilt or need for explanation.

From personal experience, blending different grief styles isn't always smooth, but leading with patience and curiosity helps. We find new ways to connect, sometimes through shared silence, sometimes through stories or rituals. This honesty and respect can transform tension into quiet solidarity, reminding us that love for our pet continues to bind us, even if we each carry it differently.

Navigating Awkward Conversations: Scripts for Friends and Coworkers

Nothing really prepares you for people's reactions when your cat dies. The news often brings awkwardness: discomfort, a quick change of subject, or careless remarks like "It was just a cat." Such words sting, even unintentionally. You may want to defend your grief without drawing attention. Most people aren't trying to hurt you; they simply don't understand. For them, pet loss might seem sad, not life-altering. For you, it's much more.

Having words ready helps. Setting boundaries doesn't mean starting arguments; sometimes, it's quietly standing up for your feelings. If someone dismisses your loss, you might say, "She was family to me, so it's a big loss." This simple response communicates your pain without inviting debate. If someone seems understanding, add, "Thank you for understanding that this is hard for me right now." You don't owe a detailed explanation, but brief phrases like these gently educate without defensiveness.

If someone insists on minimizing your grief, set a firmer boundary: "I know it can be hard to understand if you haven't had a pet like this. I just need some support right now." Or simply, "Losing her changed my daily life; I'm going through a lot." These short responses help you move the conversation along without reliving the pain.

Work brings its own challenges. You may dread going in, feeling unable to focus, or hold back tears at your desk. Sometimes, just one supportive coworker makes all the difference. If you have such a person, let them know how you're feeling. An ally can offer comfort, buffer you from insensitivity, or advocate for you if needed.

If you need time off or flexibility, don't hesitate to ask. You might tell your manager, "I've experienced a significant loss at home, and I'm struggling right now. Could I take a day off or adjust my schedule this week?" If the loss feels too personal to name, it's fine to just say you're handling a personal matter and need flexibility. If you wish to be specific, "My cat passed away, and she was a huge part of my life; I need some time," is honest and clear. Most workplaces have bereavement or mental health policies; use them if you need to.

In your social life, you'll likely face similar comments, like, "Are you still upset about your cat?" or "When will you get another pet?" Remember, not everyone can meet you emotionally where you are. Notice those who listen, or who share their own stories of loss. These people will support your grief. Don't waste energy seeking comfort from those who minimize your feelings; lean on those who show compassion.

Often, simply naming your needs is enough: "I'm having a hard time right now; could we talk about something else?" or "I'd appreciate not talking about pets today." Setting these boundaries protects you and helps others not make things harder.

Not all friends or coworkers will understand your grief. That's okay. Find one or two allies, at work or outside, who "get it," or at least respect your pain. Lean on them when you need to. If no one close to you fits, online groups or support forums often offer welcome empathy from strangers.

Quick Reference: Scripts for Tricky Moments

- "She was family to me, so this has been really tough."

- "Thank you for letting me take some time; I'm still processing everything."
- "I appreciate your patience while I get back on my feet."
- "I'd rather not talk about pets right now, I'm still adjusting."
- "This loss has changed my routine in ways I didn't expect."

Navigating these conversations takes practice and courage, but every honest answer gives you room to grieve and, maybe, helps others grow a little more compassionate.

Grief affects all of life, at home, with friends, at work, and around those who don't always understand. This chapter looked at healing with others and protecting your heart from those who struggle to relate. Next, we'll explore how community and ongoing support can comfort you even long after the initial loss.

Chapter 7

Purr Therapy for the Soul & Self-Compassion Inspired by Cats

Some mornings, the urge to get up and face the day disappears beneath a heavy cloud of sadness. You might find yourself missing not just your cat, but the easy way they took care of themselves. Cats don't agonise over whether they deserve comfort or rest; they simply claim it. When a patch of sunlight appears on the carpet, a cat doesn't hesitate. She finds her spot, circles once or twice, and settles in, letting the warmth soak into her bones. This instinct for pleasure and ease is a lesson worth following, especially when your heart is still mending.

If you watch a cat move through her day, you'll see a masterclass in self-care. After a nap, she stretches, arching her back with slow intention. She seeks out cozy corners, soft blankets, and the quiet serenity of a hidden shelf when the world feels loud. Meals are enjoyed fully, one bite at a time, with no guilt for savoring every morsel. When your cat felt tired, she rested, no questions asked. These simple acts are not selfish; they're survival. Cats honour their needs with a kind of unapologetic devotion we humans often deny ourselves.

You deserve that same gentle attention. Right now, you may feel pressure to "get over it" or jump back into old routines, but healing after loss requires patience. It's okay to let yourself be softer and slower. Allow time to rest in your own sunbeam, whatever that looks like for you. Find a chair by the window or step outside when the sun is warm. Close your eyes for two minutes and picture your cat beside you, both of you basking in quiet comfort. There's no need to rush; cats certainly wouldn't.

Start your day with a simple stretch. When you wake up, reach your arms overhead, then twist side to side. Let your body move in a way that feels good, just like your cat would after waking from a nap. Maybe even add a little wiggle to your spine and roll your shoulders back. This small act can unlock tension and give you a sense of calm before the world gets noisy. It's not about exercise or goals, it's about honouring what your body needs.

Give yourself permission to rest without guilt. Picture yourself as your own "fur baby." If you were caring for someone as tenderly as you cared for your cat, what would you offer? Would you insist they get up and be productive every minute? Or would you encourage naps in the afternoon sun, slow mornings with a warm mug, or simply the freedom to be sad? Try giving yourself that same kindness.

Guided Self-Compassion Exercise: "Fur Baby Care for You"

- Find a spot that feels safe and comfortable—maybe a favorite chair or even on the floor by a window.

- Sit or lie down and close your eyes if that feels right.

- Take three slow breaths in and out. Let each breath be as gentle as possible.

- Picture your cat curled up nearby or on your lap.

- Now ask yourself: "If I were my own fur baby today, what would I need?"

- Answer honestly, maybe it's quiet, maybe it's company, maybe it's just a glass of water or an extra blanket.

- Promise yourself to give at least one of those things before the day ends.

You might worry that this is self-indulgent or silly, but it's not. Grief is exhausting work; your body and spirit both need time to recover. Think about how your cat would treat herself: she'd find comfort without apology. She'd walk away from noise or stress and curl up somewhere soft until she felt ready to face the world again.

I've heard from readers who discovered real comfort by following their cats' lead. One man told me that after losing his tabby, he started taking guilt-free naps on weekends because that's what his cat always did when he was sad or tired. At first, he felt lazy and unproductive. But over time, he realized those naps were healing; he woke with less heaviness in his chest, more able to remember his cat with warmth instead of sharp pain. Another reader started meeting her grief each morning by sitting in the same sunbeam her cat loved most, sometimes with tears, sometimes just breathing, and found that these few minutes became an anchor in her hardest days.

Let yourself follow these instincts. Pause when you need to pause. Stretch as your cat did after sleep. Find warmth in sunlight, soft blankets, or the company of someone gentle, and soak it up without apology. When you treat yourself with the same patience you offered your cat, you remind yourself that love doesn't vanish when the body does; it lingers in every act of kindness you turn inward.

Your cat modelled self-compassion every day without guilt or shame; now it's your turn to honour their memory by caring for yourself just as fiercely.

Building a Cat-Inspired Self-Care Plan & Daily Actions for Healing

LOSING A CAT AND TRYING TO MOVE FORWARD CAN FEEL LIKE

wandering through familiar spaces with everything just a bit off. Yet, in the silence, the habits and routines you shared remain as gentle echoes, reminders that can comfort and guide you. Leaning into those shared rituals lets you weave your cat's spirit into daily acts of self-care. This isn't about forcing yourself to feel better, but about honouring your connection and creating small spaces of warmth amid the ache.

Recall the small routines you had together. Maybe your cat appeared every afternoon as you reached for a snack, or insisted on her treat at the same time each evening. Instead of skipping these moments now, use them as gentle rituals for yourself. For example, give yourself a little treat at her usual snack time, a square of chocolate, a cup of tea, or fruit, something that feels nurturing. These acts aren't just about filling time; they nourish you and maintain a thread of connection.

Movement is another comforting thread. Cats were masters of play, suddenly sprinting down the hall or leaping onto countertops. You can adapt that idea for yourself: set a timer for a "play break," and do something that shifts your energy, a few minutes of dancing, working on a puzzle, or doodling. You might even talk out loud to your cat, sharing memories or smiling at what she'd do if she were there. These small acts, however brief, root you in your body and remind you that joy and laughter are still accessible.

The senses offer powerful ties to healing. You may have a blanket or shirt still holding your cat's scent, or maybe there's a favorite chair she loved. Don't rush to put these things away. Let yourself hold onto them when you need comfort. Sound can also soothe; online playlists of gentle cat purrs and meows are available to play while you rest, read, or drift to sleep. Even faint reminders can bring surprising comfort when the house feels too quiet.

Scents are anchors, too. If your cat loved napping in warm laundry, you might wash a blanket or shirt with the same detergent, or add a drop of a calming essential oil like lavender (if safe for you). Smell can bring lost moments back vividly and turn sharp memories into something gentler.

To track how you're doing, try journaling, what I call my "purr-o-meter." Make a daily note or small doodle to show how things felt. Maybe one day is stormy, another has patches of sun. Use colors or a few words to record the day, perhaps noting what helped or what didn't. This isn't for judgment, just a gentle record to witness your progress and patterns.

Consistency helps these self-care rituals stick, but they don't have to be complex. Simple checklists are an easy lifeline for low-motivation days. Here's a cat-inspired example:

Cat-Inspired Self-Care Checklist

- Sat in a sunny spot (even briefly)
- Wrapped up in my softest blanket
- Listened to calming sounds (music or purrs)
- Enjoyed a treat at snack time
- Took a playful break (danced, drew, did a puzzle)
- Smelled something comforting (laundry, candle)
- Noted my mood on the "purr-o-meter"
- Spoke aloud one memory or affirmation

Check what fits each day. Some days you might manage only one; other days, several. The goal isn't perfection, but gentle forward movement, honouring both your longing and your hope. Each act is a quiet tribute to your cat, and to your own strength in healing.

Over time, you'll find which comforts help most and which routines brighten your days. By leaning into these cat-inspired habits, you begin to rebuild, slowly. Each snack, play moment, or sunlit pause becomes a way of sustaining yourself; grief doesn't vanish, but the love you shared continues in small, caring acts.

Mindful Moments and Meditations: Remembering with Gratitude

Grief likes to pull the mind into yesterday or tomorrow, a replay of what's lost, a worry about what's next. It's easy to get stuck in that loop, but there's another way to soften the ache: mindfulness. This isn't about clearing your head of pain or pretending you don't miss your cat; it's about pausing to notice small things right now. Mindfulness gives sorrow a place to rest, but it also lets gratitude walk in the door. You can hold both feelings at once. Cats seemed to know this secret already, how to be entirely present, whether curled into your lap or batting at a string. They didn't fret about time slipping away. They just soaked up the moment, and you can do the same, one breath at a time.

When you want to remember your cat with gentleness, try a short meditation with a feline twist. Start by sitting somewhere quiet, maybe where your cat liked to nap. Close your eyes and breathe slowly and deeply. Picture a favorite "meowmory", perhaps the way your cat blinked sleepily when you read at night, or the sound of their purr rumbling against your chest. As you inhale, imagine drawing in that warmth and comfort; as you exhale, let your shoulders drop, letting out tension with every breath. Visualize your cat's presence nearby, not gone, just changed, woven into the soft texture of memory. You might feel sadness well up, and that's okay. Let tears fall if they come; they're just another way your heart honours love.

You don't have to set aside hours for this practice. Even a minute or two can make an impact. If you prefer audio, there are gentle guided meditations online, some even include soft purring or calming music designed for grieving pet owners. Use headphones and give yourself permission to step away from chores or screens while you listen. Sometimes, sitting still feels impossible. That's fine too. You can be mindful while doing dishes or folding laundry. Just pause for a heartbeat and notice one thing: the warmth of water on your hands, the quiet in your living room, the light shifting across the floor. Each of these small moments is a tribute to your cat, a silent "thank you" for the comfort they brought into your life.

Building gratitude into daily life doesn't require grand gestures; it lives in ordinary acts. Just noticing something soft, a blanket, a patch of sun, the hush before dusk, can spark a feeling of appreciation. When you walk past your cat's favorite window, pause for three breaths. Remember a time you watched birds together or shared a slow afternoon in that spot. Speak or think the words: "I'm grateful for this." If it feels forced at first, keep going. Gratitude is like a muscle; it gets stronger with gentle use.

Journaling can help ground these feelings when thoughts whirl too fast. It doesn't have to be poetic or long-winded, just honest. Try keeping a gratitude journal specifically for your cat's legacy. Each day, jot down one thing you're thankful for because of them or one memory that still makes you smile. Maybe it's as simple as "Today, I remembered how she'd greet me at the door" or "I'm grateful for every silly leap onto the kitchen counter." These entries may seem small, but over time they become a mosaic of love and comfort, a quiet affirmation that your bond endures.

Prompts can get you started if words don't come easily:

- "One thing my cat taught me about happiness is..."
- "Today I felt close to my cat when..."
- "I'm thankful for this memory: ___________."
- "My cat's favorite game always made me laugh because..."

Some days, gratitude flows easily; other days it hides under grief's shadow. There's no need to chase it down, just look for tiny glimmers where you can. You might find yourself pausing in the middle of routine tasks, suddenly aware of how lucky you were to have loved and been loved by such a companion. That realization doesn't erase loss, but it does shift something inside you—a bit more space for hope, a touch more room for peace.

In time, this practice becomes almost second nature. You'll catch yourself smiling at sunlight on the wall or a stray cat outside, not because you've moved on but because you remember what it felt like to share those simple joys with your own fur friend. Each mindful moment is another stitch in the fabric of healing, loose and imperfect, but strong enough to hold both sorrow and thanks.

Re-entering Old Spaces—Returning to the Vet, Pet Store, or Favorite Spot

Walking into the vet's office after losing your cat is a moment few want to face. The familiar smells, the posters of kittens, and the gentle sounds all now feel different. Your chest may tighten, or anxious memories may resurface, sometimes just from driving by. These strong reactions are completely normal; revisiting places connected with your cat can bring back sadness, anger, or a mix of tangled emotions. Many avoid these spots for weeks or months, worried it might unravel their healing. Feeling this dread doesn't mean weakness; it simply reflects deep love.

Preparing ahead can help. Don't go alone if it's too much; ask someone to come along, even if only to offer silent support. Remind yourself of your reason for returning, like another pet's checkup or picking up supplies. Set a small, manageable goal for the visit, maybe just refilling medication. Limit your time: handle only the essentials. If emotion overwhelms you there, it's okay to step outside and breathe. No one expects composure.

Pet stores bring their own challenges. You may reflexively reach for your cat's favorite treat, only to pause. The toy aisle might feel like a museum of memories. When you need to shop for another pet or a friend, make a plan. Go during quiet hours, stick to a list, and avoid aisles that feel especially raw at first. Skipping a difficult section isn't failure, it's self-care.

Hardest of all are spots at home: a sunny patch your cat loved, or an old chair she claimed. Sitting there again can feel sacred. Mark these moments with personal rituals. Consider lighting a candle before and after your outing, or jot down your thoughts on how it felt. Simple affirmations like "I made it through" or "That was hard, but I did it" can offer comfort. Rituals won't erase the pain, but they honour your courage.

Unexpected encounters may happen: a receptionist who remembers your cat, a casual question from a store clerk, or another pet owner's friendly chat. These can take you off guard. Having a simple phrase ready helps: "This is my first time back since I lost my cat, so I might be a bit emotional." Most people will offer understanding, or at least space. If pressed for details, "I'm still adjusting, it's a tough time" is enough.

Acknowledge each step, no matter how small, whether you dash into the clinic or sit for moments in a favorite chair. These are acts of quiet bravery, showing that grief changes you, but doesn't control your life.

If intense emotion hits afterwards, tears in the parking lot, anger at home, don't judge yourself. Feel what you need to feel; these responses are simply the mixture of love and loss. Over time, these visits may become easier. For now, every step counts, even if it just means walking past and not stopping.

Writing a few sentences about your experience can help release tension. Note what surprised you; perhaps it was easier or harder than you'd thought. Treat these notes as progress, not setbacks. Returning to familiar places isn't about leaving grief behind but about letting sadness and healing coexist, allowing old memories to blend with new ones without rush or shame.

Take as long as you need before going back, or decide it's not time yet. This process is yours alone; you set the pace.

When Is It "Okay" to Love Again? Thinking About a New Cat

THE ACHE OF LOSING A CAT LINGERS IN WAYS THAT SOMETIMES FEEL endless. You might catch yourself glancing at adoption pages online, feeling a tug of hope mixed with guilt, or maybe you avoid even thinking about another pet for fear it means letting go. This is such a complicated spot to be in, yearning for that unique companionship, but feeling as though you're somehow betraying the cat you lost. I've been there too, and I know firsthand how tangled the feelings get. It's common to wonder if bringing a new cat home means you're moving on too soon, or replacing a relationship that can never really be replaced. These are questions with no easy answers, and yet, the heart keeps quietly asking them.

You're not alone in this struggle, and there's nothing wrong with feeling torn. The idea of loving again can stir up anxiety, relief, or even anger at yourself. Sometimes it feels like you're standing at the edge of a pool, testing the water with your toe, not sure if you'll sink or swim. There's no "right" time to open your home or your heart again. For some, the urge springs up quickly, a quiet house feels unbearable, and the comfort of a warm body or a familiar purr helps soften the sharpest edges of grief. For others, the space left behind is sacred, not ready to be filled by another presence for months, years, or maybe ever.

It helps to ask yourself some honest questions without judgment or pressure. Pause and reflect: Am I looking for a new cat to escape loneliness, or am I ready to share new love? Do I hope another cat will fill the exact space my old one left behind, or am I open to a whole new story? What would my late cat want for me? Would she want me to stay closed off, or would she hope I found warmth and company again? These aren't questions with neat answers, but letting them sit in your mind can provide clarity over time.

I've spoken with people who adopted again almost immediately after loss. For one woman, the silence at home was too much; adopting a young rescue just weeks later didn't erase her grief, but gave her small reasons to get up and move each day. She told me she still talked to her late cat's photo while feeding the new kitten, and that felt right, not wrong. Another friend waited years before considering another pet. Every time he thought about visiting the shelter, he'd remember his cat's quirks, a particular way of jumping on the counter for treats, and back away. Eventually, he realised that his life had shifted so much that he didn't need to adopt again; instead, he started volunteering at a rescue, finding a connection without bringing a new cat home. Some people choose never to adopt again, and that's an act of love too, honouring what was special about their bond by letting it stand alone.

If you do feel ready, or even just curious, about welcoming a new cat, it can help to create space for both love and memory. You aren't erasing your cat's legacy by opening your heart again; you're expanding it. Setting up a "legacy shelf" is one way to respect both chapters. Find a spot at home for cherished mementoes, a favorite toy, a collar, a framed photo, maybe even a letter you wrote after saying goodbye. This becomes a gentle reminder that your first cat will always be part of your story, no matter who else arrives in your life.

Naming rituals can be healing as well. Some choose names that echo their old cat, while others pick something entirely different as a marker of new beginnings. There's no shame in telling friends or family that this decision carries mixed emotions. You might even talk aloud to your late cat as you prepare the home for another, letting her know she'll always have her place.

No matter what you decide or when you decide it, please give yourself permission to feel everything: anticipation, worry, excitement, nostalgia. All these feelings belong. If guilt surfaces when joy bubbles up, remind yourself that love isn't finite; it grows and multiplies with every act of care. You're not replacing anyone, you're opening your heart in tribute to all the love you've already known and given.

When you welcome a new cat, grieve openly if tears come as you watch her curl into an old bed or chase shadows down the hall. Let laughter and longing mingle without shame. If you choose not to adopt again, honour that wisdom too; there are many ways to keep your late cat's memory alive without adding a new companion.

This decision is yours alone. Take all the time you need; trust that love will find its way into your life again in whatever form suits you best.

Finding Joy Without Guilt & Letting Yourself Smile Again

It can feel strange, even uncomfortable, the first time you catch yourself smiling after losing your cat. The idea that grief and joy are mutually exclusive is persistent. You might worry that laughter means you're forgetting, or that a good day is a betrayal. But here's what I've learned: joy and sorrow aren't rivals; they're simply neighbors in your heart. Smiling doesn't erase the love you carry. Laughter doesn't fade memories. Instead, these moments show your cat's lasting presence in your life by proving that their spirit, playful, curious, loving, still shapes your world.

Consider what made your cat happy: batting at a paper ball, napping in the sun, chasing a string. Cats embrace pleasure without apology. To honour your cat's legacy, allow yourself to welcome joy back in, not as a way of moving on, but as a tribute. You might volunteer at a shelter, spending time with cats in need, dedicating your efforts to your cat's memory. Every gentle touch or purr becomes a living legacy. Or maybe host a small cat-themed gathering with understanding friends. Share stories, use silly cat mugs, and toast all the whiskered companions who've brightened your life. These actions don't replace what you lost; they keep the spirit of delight alive.

Finding joy takes practice after loss. At first, happiness may feel fleeting, a bright moment watching birds or seeing your favorite flower bloom. These small sparks matter. Notice when they appear. Pause, and let yourself feel them, even if sadness follows. Use simple prompts to anchor yourself: "When I laugh today, I'll remember how my cat brought joy into my life." Or, "When something warms my heart, I'll let it remind me of all the good my cat brought." These reminders don't force you to be happy. They help you recognize that happiness is not an enemy of grief.

Guilt might surface when you start to feel better. You may think, "Shouldn't I still be sad?" But your cat wouldn't want you stuck in pain forever. When guilt creeps in, repeat mantras like: "My happiness honours my cat's memory." Or simply, "It's okay to feel good again." You may need these affirmations often, say them out loud, write them down, or send them as texts to yourself. Let them shield you against old, limiting beliefs about grieving.

Letting joy in can feel vulnerable. I've had days when I laughed with friends but cried alone later, conflicted about enjoying anything while hurting. Over time, I learned these feelings can coexist. Laughter softens grief and makes it easier to breathe. Savoring small pleasures, a good meal, a funny video, the company of kind people, felt like my cat cheering me on from some sunlit memory.

Try creating rituals that blend remembrance with celebration. Light a candle before doing something fun, dedicating your happiness to your cat's spirit. Or share a happy memory at dinner with supportive people. Such acts bridge loss and life, showing that love leaves lasting echoes, which don't fade when you let yourself live fully again.

Notice how your body feels when you smile or laugh. Do you feel lighter? Let that feeling be. Each happy moment weaves another thread into your story with your cat, a story with hard goodbyes, but also endless moments of delight.

Grief won't ask you to forget or "move on." It asks you to keep moving, even in small steps. Joy isn't a finish line; it's another hue in the tapestry of memory and love.

As this chapter closes, allow yourself to welcome happiness again, not to replace grief, but to accompany it. Your smiles, laughter, and celebrations do not diminish your loss; they expand the reach of your cat's love, showing that healing and connection are always possible. In the next chapter, we'll look at how community and support can sustain you through all the seasons of remembrance and renewal.

Chapter 8

Finding Your People: Pet Loss Support Groups and Online Communities

When you lose a cat, the world moves on, often oblivious to your pain. Grief can feel isolating, as though only you carry the weight. Yet, there are entire networks of people, quiet strangers and potential friends, who know this same loss and are eager to support you. They don't shy away when you mention "fur babies"; they understand references to phantom purrs and sleep disrupted by a missing jingle. These are the people who truly get it.

When you connect with others who understand, you find relief in not needing to justify your sorrow or explain why seeing an empty food bowl derails your afternoon. While general bereavement groups exist, there's something intimate about sharing with other cat lovers. The shared understanding of the cat-human bond means you don't have to defend your grief. In these spaces, your bond and sorrow are honoured and spoken in a familiar language; this shared empathy lightens your load.

Support options now are as varied as our cats themselves. If you seek in-person connection, local humane societies or veterinary clinics often host pet loss support groups, gentle spaces for stories and understanding, sometimes with a counsellor, often with someone who's been through it. If leaving home is hard, virtual communities provide comfort from your couch. Some groups specialize, for those who lost senior cats or those grappling with medical decision guilt, so you can find what resonates most.

Online, options abound. Moderated Facebook groups and subreddits like r/petloss provide open, supportive spaces for sharing memories, venting, or marking meaningful moments. Many offer privacy; users often join with pseudonyms and participate in whatever way feels safe, reading before ever posting. For a quieter space, online memorial sites let you honour your cat with photos, virtual candles, and guestbooks, creating a ritual and a sense of permanence, especially comforting on tough anniversaries.

Choosing a support group while grieving can be overwhelming, so take it slow. Start by reading posts and getting a feel for the community. Some groups are light and filled with memes; others offer deep listening and gentle support. Prefer anonymity? Set up an account with a nickname for added safety, giving you room to share openly without worry about coworkers or relatives finding your posts. Set personal boundaries; it's fine to log off if something feels too heavy or triggering.

How you participate is entirely up to you: posting a photo, commenting, just "liking," or only reading others' stories. You might eventually share advice or encouragement, but you may simply find comfort in knowing others echo your feelings. "Lurking", just reading, is a perfectly valid form of participation. Many find solace in seeing their own emotions reflected.

Remarkably, these communities often yield deep connections. For example, one person joined a small online forum after losing her tabby and found herself exchanging supportive emails with another mourner across the country. Their friendship, born of shared grief, grew to include everyday joys, a reminder that even loss can lead to new, meaningful bonds.

Some groups hold virtual candlelight vigils on difficult anniversaries or holidays when pet loss feels toughest. People from various places log in together, each lighting a candle for their cat while sharing names. The screen fills with candlelight, a moving testament to enduring connection and remembrance across distances.

Reflection Section: Finding Your Comfort Zone

Take five minutes to jot down what feels supportive to you now. Do you want quiet observation, active sharing, local events, online chats, or one-on-one exchanges? List three qualities or boundaries you want, perhaps privacy, kindness, or the freedom not to participate, and let these guide you in choosing your space.

Finding your people is less about sympathy and more about belonging, knowing your grief is seen, honoured, and understood. Among fellow cat lovers, healing may not be immediate, but in these supportive circles, it finally feels possible.

Sharing Your Story & How to Give and Receive Comfort

Telling your story can be like opening a window after days of gloom, air and light enter where before there was only heaviness. Whether you describe your cat's last days or the funny things that made them unique, sharing grief can ease the burden. It's not about seeking applause or advice, but about being witnessed in your truth. Many people keep pain to themselves, fearing it's too much for others. But voicing your memories, spoken, written, or shared in a photo, can reduce isolation and help transform private grief into something lighter.

A good way to start is with a prompt like "My cat taught me..." Your answer might be practical (enjoying a sunny spot or never ignoring a closed door) or something deeper, like patience or unconditional love. These insights matter. Another way in is to capture a "meowmory"—a vivid moment that sums up your bond. It could be how your cat curled up with you as you read or chirped at birds through the window. Recording these memories in a notebook, online, or with a friend can turn loss into legacy. Don't worry about being poetic; honesty is enough. Some people start small, with just a sentence or a single image or memory.

Listening to others is as important as sharing your own story. If someone opens up about losing their cat, your role isn't to fix their pain but to truly listen. People may rush to give advice, suggesting new routines or adopting another pet, but most grievers just want to be heard. Simple acknowledgements like "I hear you," or "That sounds so hard," show you respect their pain. You don't need to relate your own experience, just stay present. Tears, yours or theirs, are okay. Support can also mean silent company; sometimes, quietly sitting together helps most.

If you're not sure how to respond to someone's loss, recall what comforted you (or what you wish someone had offered). Phrases like "Your love for her is so clear," or "Thank you for trusting me with this," matter. Try not to compare losses, cheer them up too soon, or push them to move on. Every grief is its own world and deserves respect.

Comfort is a two-way street; you can give and receive it, even when you feel empty yourself. Sending a sympathy card to someone grieving the loss of a pet can mean a lot. Even simple messages like "Thinking of you and your beautiful cat" carry weight. Online, look for forums or social media threads where people share memories or comforting words about their cats. You can contribute your own story or just offer kind responses like, "What a lovely spirit she had," or "Thank you for sharing his story."

Building community through support doesn't require grand gestures. Sometimes, it's as simple as reacting to a post with a heart emoji or replying with your own memory. In person, you might bring cookies to a friend who's grieving, or just share time and quiet company. Every small act becomes part of a patchwork of kindness that helps many people heal.

If you want to share your story but don't know where to start, here are some prompts:

Story Prompts for Comfort and Connection

- My cat taught me...
- The silliest thing my cat ever did was...
- What I miss most is...
- A memory that always makes me smile...
- If I could tell my cat one thing now, it would be...

You can use these prompts in a journal, online, as sticky notes around your home, or spoken aloud in private. Every gesture matters; every word honours your love and helps you and others feel less alone.

By reaching out, sharing your story, or supporting someone else, you help weave a tapestry of remembrance that stretches far beyond your own home. Every voice adds to a shared comfort that endures long after the telling.

Gentle Approaches to Spirituality: Rainbow Bridge and Beyond

When grief over losing a beloved cat feels overwhelming, it's natural to seek meaning—some sense that your cat's presence continues beyond death. The Rainbow Bridge is a comforting idea for many: a peaceful, sunny meadow where pets, healthy and joyful, await reunion with those they loved. Some people find deep solace in imagining their cat thriving at the Rainbow Bridge; others see it as a gentle story rather than a fact. What matters most is whether the metaphor brings you comfort. For some, it softens the pain of loss and offers hope; for others, comfort may come from believing love lives on in memory or in nature, without the need for a defined afterlife.

Beliefs about what happens after death are as varied as cats' personalities. You may draw from a religious background or a more practical, nonspiritual outlook. All of these perspectives are welcome; what's most important is what soothes your heart. If the Rainbow Bridge resonates with you, embrace the image of your cat at peace, waiting in a beautiful place. If it doesn't, there are countless other ways to honour the enduring connection you feel. Individual comfort should guide your expressions of grief, not anyone else's script.

Many find solace in simple rituals. Some light a candle at sunset, sending love "to the stars" for their cat. Others write letters and tuck them into a "heavenly mailbox," whether it's a box, a drawer, or even a tree hollow. These personal acts aren't about asserting what happens after death; instead, they give your love a place to go. Talking aloud to your cat when the house is quiet, or whispering goodnight before sleep, can become comforting routines. Such gestures let you express your love privately, without needing anyone's approval.

In my own family, we talk openly about loved ones living on in memory. We might say, "She's in the sunshine," or "He's part of every happy moment." There's no insistence on what's "right"; everyone finds language that feels true for them. One friend tells her children their cat "became a story in our hearts," while another describes it as energy returning to the world. Respect, not dogma, does the most healing in these matters.

If tangible acts help, consider a "wish jar", a glass container or decorated box for notes to your cat: brief messages, funny memories, or questions you wish you could ask. Over time, these notes create a tapestry of love and remembrance. On meaningful dates, your cat's birthday, adoption day, or their passing, you can revisit the jar, reading old notes or adding new ones.

A gentle ritual some choose is a remembrance walk on a significant day.

Walk a route your cat enjoyed or another peaceful place. Bring a small token, such as a stone or flower, and leave it in a spot that feels right as a tribute. Go alone or with loved ones; either way, this act becomes a quiet link between your memories and the present, honouring what was, without fuss or explanation.

Remembrance doesn't have to be spiritual or solemn. Creating art can be healing, painting stones, making collages, writing poems, or planting flowers or trees in your cat's memory. Even sharing stories over dinner keeps your cat's spirit alive, as laughter and tears mingle around shared memories.

Ultimately, choose words and rituals that comfort, not constrain, your heart. If something doesn't feel right, try something else or create your own tradition. Grief and remembrance are deeply personal. In every form, spiritual or not, honouring your cat is an act of love, not of doctrine. Choose the language and rituals that best fit you and your family; all beliefs and hopes are valid in this space.

Ritual Exercise: Lighting the Way

One evening this week, light a candle in your cat's honour. As the flame flickers, share aloud (or quietly) a favorite memory or a hope for your cat, whether you envision them at the Rainbow Bridge, among the stars, or always in your heart. Let this light be a symbol that love endures, no matter what you believe comes next.

Creating New Traditions: Annual Rituals of Remembrance

Repetition carries a quiet strength. As the date of your cat's adoption or passing approaches each year, you may feel both longing and warmth. Honouring these days with a ritual, no matter how simple, helps give your feelings a place and creates a pause to celebrate the connection that shaped your life. These annual traditions aren't meant to prolong grief, but to support intentional remembering and allow love to be acknowledged openly rather than hidden. With time, such rituals become steady markers through the years, blending joy and sadness, and reminding you that remembering is courageous.

You can begin with small gestures: placing a single flower by your cat's photo, enjoying a treat in their honour, or repeating a beloved tradition each "gotcha day", the anniversary of your cat coming home. Lighting a candle, reading a poem, or playing a favorite song can ground you in memory. Some gather close friends or family for a "cat celebration day," sharing stories and laughter, perhaps by baking a treat that reminds them of their pet. Others give back by making a yearly donation to a rescue group or shelter, turning remembrance into compassion for animals in need.

Rituals are as individual as the cats we celebrate. Some mark the first bright day of spring by adding to a memory garden, a single daffodil the first year, then more flowers each spring, building a living tribute. Others host an annual picnic for animal lovers to swap stories and photos, transforming a private remembrance into a cherished community tradition.

These rituals can change and grow alongside you. Early on, you may only manage the smallest act, a quiet toast, a note tucked under a pillow, or a few reflective moments. As time passes and your relationship with grief evolves, you might create bigger remembrances: organizing group walks, painting memory stones, or making a special meal and sharing a toast of gratitude for all those table scraps and companionship.

Personal touches matter most. What's meaningful is what feels authentic to you, not what tradition dictates. As new memories form, your rituals may shift: a single tealight one year, music or friends joining in the next. Involve children or other pets if you wish, letting them contribute with drawings, treats, or flowers for the garden. The purpose isn't perfection, but being present.

Notice what brings comfort and what feels forced. There's no rulebook: it's okay to skip a year or change traditions as your needs shift. Grief ebbs and flows, and so can your rituals for honouring what was lost and what endures.

Some plant seeds with symbolic meaning each anniversary, letting the evolving garden mirror their own healing. Others watch home videos together, sharing laughter over old antics, or write an annual letter reflecting on the changes since their cat's passing, then read it aloud in a meaningful place.

For those who find peace in quiet reflection, sipping coffee in your cat's favorite spot and watching the light shift can be enough. If you find comfort in action, volunteering or fundraising for animals on significant dates can offer a sense of purpose.

If you ever question whether your way of remembering is "enough," trust yourself, your ritual just needs to fit your heart. Start small: one flower, a meaningful song, or simply saying your cat's name aloud on their day. Over time, these traditions stitch themselves into the fabric of your life, a gentle reminder that love always remains.

Some rituals may fade over the years; others deepen. That's natural. Healing changes, and remembrance needn't be scripted. Year after year, these traditions invite you to honour both joy and sorrow, a celebration of everything your cat brought into your life and everything you still carry forward.

Advocating for Yourself & Responding to "It's Just a Cat"

You may have noticed that the world doesn't always make room for the kind of grief that comes with losing a beloved cat. People say things that sting, often without intending to cause harm. Someone might shrug and tell you, "It's just a cat," as if your heart should rebound right away. When this happens, something inside can shut down. You might start to question your own feelings or hide your sadness to avoid being dismissed. But your sorrow deserves respect; your cat was family, not just a footnote in your life. Standing up for that truth is not only brave, it's also necessary for your healing.

Pushing back against these comments doesn't mean starting a fight or trying to win someone over. It means protecting your own experience, setting boundaries, and being honest about what you need. If someone tells you to get over it or acts puzzled by your tears, you don't have to convince them of anything. Sometimes, a simple statement like, "She was my family," or "This loss is real for me," draws a clear but gentle line. You're not asking for permission to grieve, you're stating a fact about your own life. If you want to share more, you might add, "I know not everyone understands, but she was there for me in ways most people never saw." That's enough. Your story stands on its own.

Choosing when and how to engage is your right. Sometimes it's worth explaining; other times, protecting your peace matters more. There are moments when someone's ignorance just isn't worth your energy. You get to decide, on the spot or later, if you want to open up or keep things private. For acquaintances or coworkers who don't seem to get it, try: "I appreciate your concern, but it helps me to talk about her." This phrase is assertive but not aggressive; it signals what you need without asking for approval. If you're not in the mood to discuss, you can say, "I'd rather not talk about this right now, but thank you for understanding." That closes the door with kindness and keeps you in control.

Advocating for yourself also means knowing which conversations are worth having. With some people, close friends, partners, maybe even a boss, you might want to educate gently. It's okay to say, "Losing her has been harder than I expected. She was more than a pet; she was part of my daily life." Most people don't realize how deep these bonds run until they hear it from someone they care about. Sometimes, these honest moments plant seeds that grow into empathy over time.

There are also opportunities for bigger change when you speak up. Not long ago, a reader told me about her experience at work after her cat died. She took a personal day because she couldn't face the office without falling apart. When her manager questioned her absence, she explained how much her cat meant to her and how hard it was getting through the day pretending everything was fine. Instead of shutting down, she described the routines they shared and what she'd lost. Her courage started a real conversation in the workplace about pet loss and grief. Within a few months, her company introduced a policy allowing pet bereavement leave, a small but important step toward recognizing this unique pain as legitimate.

These moments of self-advocacy ripple outward. When you name your grief or ask for support, others notice. You may quietly or loudly give permission for someone else to do the same when their time comes. Sometimes the world changes slowly; sometimes it shifts with a single honest sentence spoken at the right moment.

You don't have to educate everyone or justify your feelings to every person who crosses your path. Still, finding language that feels true for you is powerful armour against a society that sometimes forgets how much cats matter. Practice saying what feels right in front of a mirror or write down phrases that help you hold your ground. If words fail in the moment, remember there is no shame in circling back later with an email or text: "Just wanted to clarify how important she was in my life."

None of this is easy, especially when emotions are raw, and words come slowly. But every time you advocate for yourself, even in a small way, you honour both your cat and your own heart. You remind yourself (and maybe the world) that love should never be minimized, no matter who receives it or what form it takes.

Carrying Their Love Forward: Living Well With Whisker Memories

Long after your cat is gone, their presence echoes in simple moments: pausing in a sunbeam, stretching out leisurely, or watching birds, habits once shared. These everyday reminders aren't just about missing them; they're invitations to live more intentionally and warmly. Many people grapple with how to hold on to their cat's love without being overwhelmed by absence. Often, the answer is to channel that love into action, letting your cat's memory inspire joy, connection, and purpose.

A meaningful way to honour their memory is by choosing kindness in their name. Volunteering at an animal shelter, especially with cats needing patience and care, lets you share the love you still have. This isn't about replacing your cat but spreading the affection they gave you. Supporting local TNR groups or fostering kittens offers a sense of purpose and lets your cat's legacy live on through good deeds. Even if you can't volunteer regularly, simple gestures like donating supplies or supporting animal causes online can help you give back and keep your cat's spirit close.

Honouring your cat's legacy isn't limited to organizations. Teaching a child about gentleness, perhaps by sharing stories of your cat's trust or your own patience, shapes hearts for years ahead. Children learn deeply from such examples, absorbing kindness and empathy from your words and actions. Small, daily acts, checking on a neighbor's pet, rescuing a stray, or leaving water out for animals, also become quiet gestures of remembrance, each one a tribute to your cat's influence.

"Whisker memories", those tiny, unexpected flashes of recall, don't have to hurt forever. Over time, they offer comfort, a persistent reminder that love endures. Keeping a journal or blog focused on positive memories allows you to revisit the best moments whenever you need them. Collecting favorite stories, quotes, photos, or sketches brings gratitude into daily life and helps balance joy and sorrow. Revisiting these memories during hard moments can offer strength, even sparking a needed smile.

Your bond with your cat doesn't disappear; it evolves. Some take comfort in jewellery engraved with their cat's name or paw print, a subtle support on tough days. Others reflect on a "legacy list", reminders of lessons their cat taught: patience, resilience, the joy of sunlight. When life is difficult, reading this list can provide grounding and clarity, showing how your cat's wisdom endures long after they're gone.

Creativity can also help memorialize your cat. Create art based on your cat's unique traits, a painting of their favorite napping spot, a playful comic about their zoomies, or a poem about their everyday adventures. Some plant herbs or flowers in their memory, tending these living tributes as the seasons change. You might invent a recipe inspired by your cat's favorite treat and share it with friends, making remembrance both light-hearted and meaningful.

Living well with whisker memories means letting their influence make you better. Your outlook shifts. Maybe you're a bit more patient, kinder to yourself and others, or more joyful in old routines. The way you greet each day, navigate challenges, or seek comfort is shaped by what your cat brought to your life.

Letting love continue in new forms doesn't erase sadness; it weaves the past and present together, allowing your cat's influence to grow with you. When grief feels overwhelming, these small acts, volunteering, teaching, and journaling, can ground you in hope. Through them, your cat's spirit remains not just in thought, but in action.

Moving forward, your relationship with your cat endures, sometimes clear, sometimes a soft whisper of comfort. Their lessons live on in the choices you make and how you love now.

Carrying your cat's love forward shapes how you treat others and care for yourself. Through kindness, creativity, and reflection, you keep their spirit near, turning memories into soothing companions rather than sharp reminders. These new habits and perspectives are part of the healing process and help make life richer after loss.

Conclusion

If you're reading this, you've made it through some of the hardest pages you may ever turn. Before anything else, I want to say this again, as clearly as I can: your grief is real. It's not an exaggeration, not a weakness, not "just about a pet." It's love, stretching across the gap where your cat used to be. Please let yourself believe this, especially on days when the world seems to forget. I see you, and I honour the depth of what you've lost and the strength it takes to feel it.

You have walked through memories and rituals, guilt and relief, laughter and tears. We've talked about the ways cats become family, not just pets, but witnesses to our lives, comforters, playmates, and confidants. Their absence is sharp because their presence was so woven into your days. Maybe you still expect to hear the jingle of a collar or see a tail flick past the doorway. If so, you are not alone.

This book has been about more than how to "move on." We explored why the loss of a cat can hit so deeply, and why the world sometimes doesn't understand. We talked about the rollercoaster of emotions you might feel: guilt, anger, relief, gratitude, and even flashes of joy. and how each one has a place. I hope you've found practical tools for managing the daily triggers: the empty food bowl, the silent windowsill, the nighttime ache. I hope you tried a few exercises, whether it was writing a goodbye letter, building a "Nine Lives Timeline," or just lighting a candle in the quiet. We talked about helping children and partners, supporting your other pets, and finding comfort in small routines. We looked at creative memorials, annual rituals, and ways to keep your cat's story alive. We discussed how to reach out for support and how to stand up for your right to grieve.

Here are the truths I hope you'll carry forward: There is no single "right" way to mourn a cat. Your love was unique, so your grief will be too. You don't have to rush. You don't have to explain. Love endures, even after goodbye. Healing takes time, and you are allowed to heal at your own pace. Even if you feel alone, you aren't, not really. Others have walked this path, and many stand ready to walk alongside you.

Just by picking up this book, you've shown courage. You've let yourself remember, you've tried new ways to honour your cat, and you've dared to hope for peace. Maybe you started a memory journal. Maybe you allowed yourself to laugh at a silly story, or you let yourself cry in the middle of the night. Every step counts. Every act of remembrance is a victory. Every day you choose to carry your cat's memory with kindness is a day you honour both their life and your own heart.

I can't promise that the pain will fully disappear. But I do believe that gentler days will come. Joy is still possible, even when you think you've forgotten how to find it. Your cat's love and legacy can live on in your actions, your stories, and the warmth you bring to others, whether you open your home to another animal someday or simply let "whisker memories" brighten your morning coffee.

Keep telling your stories. Mark the special days in whatever way feels right. Share a photo online, plant a flower, or light a candle. Let your rituals change with you. If you need company, seek out pet loss communities, online or in person. Don't hesitate to ask for help, whether that's talking to a friend, joining a support group, or just letting yourself be heard. The resource section at the end of this book is there for you, full of ideas, organizations, and communities where your grief will be honoured, and your cat's memory celebrated.

If you ever feel dismissed or misunderstood, remember that you have the right to advocate for your grief. Your love was not small, and neither is your loss. You matter. The bond between you and your cat matters. I hope you'll carry that truth with you, no matter what anyone else says.

Thank you for trusting me with your story, even if we've never met. Thank you for letting me walk beside you for a little while on this hard, beautiful path. Your courage, your memories, your willingness to love so deeply, it all inspires me. I am always rooting for you.

As you close this book, I hope you feel just a little lighter. Not because the grief is gone, but because you know you can carry it. You can carry your cat's love forward, in your own way, for as long as you need. The sun will rise, and there will be new moments of joy, laughter, and connection, even as you hold tight to the memories that shaped you.

Your story, and your cat's story, continue. Whisker memories are forever. Love does not end; it only changes shape. And you, dear reader, are living proof of that enduring, everyday magic.

Sources & Further Reading

Web references were accurate at the time of publication.

- Ahead App. (n.d.). *5 sacred rituals for coping with loss of a cat while healing your heart.* https://ahead-app.com/blog/Grief/5-sacred-rituals-for-coping-with-loss-of-cat-while-healing-your-hearthttps://ahead-app.com/blog/Grief/5-sacred-rituals-for-coping-with-loss-of-cat-while-healing-your-heart

- American Academy of Child and Adolescent Psychiatry. (n.d.). *When a pet dies.* https://www.aacap.org/AACAP/Families_and_Youth/Facts_for_Families/FFF-Guide/When-A-Pet-Dies-078.aspxhttps://www.aacap.org/AACAP/Families_and_Youth/Facts_for_Families/FFF-Guide/When-A-Pet-Dies-078.aspx

- American Veterinary Medical Association. (n.d.). *Coping with the loss of a pet.* https://www.avma.org/resources-tools/pet-owners/petcare/coping-loss-pethttps://www.avma.org/resources-tools/pet-owners/petcare/coping-loss-pet

- Association for Pet Loss and Bereavement. (n.d.). *Pet loss support.* https://www.aplb.org/https://www.aplb.org/

- Blue Cross. (n.d.). *Saying goodbye to your cat.* https://www.bluecross.org.uk/advice/cat/wellbeing-and-care/time-to-say-goodbye-to-your-cathttps://www.bluecross.org.uk/advice/cat/wellbeing-and-care/time-to-say-goodbye-to-your-cat

- Blue Cross. (n.d.). *Goodbye my friend: A story of pet loss.* https://

- www.bluecross.org.uk/story/goodbye-my-friend-a-story-of-pet-losshttps://www.bluecross.org.uk/story/goodbye-my-friend-a-story-of-pet-loss

- Cat Wisdom 101. (n.d.). *How to create a pet memorial garden in your backyard.*https://catwisdom101.com/how-to-create-a-diy-pet-memorial-garden-in-your-backyard/https://catwisdom101.com/how-to-create-a-diy-pet-memorial-garden-in-your-backyard/

- Class Act Cats. (n.d.). *How to support someone after their cat dies.*https://classactcats.com/blog/support-someone-after-their-cat-dies/https://classactcats.com/blog/support-someone-after-their-cat-dies/

- Dr. Scott Eilers. (n.d.). *Practical psychological strategies for coping with pet loss.*https://www.drscotteilers.com/post/practical-psychological-strategies-for-coping-with-pet-losshttps://www.drscotteilers.com/post/practical-psychological-strategies-for-coping-with-pet-loss

- Forever In My Heart Pet Loss Counselling. (n.d.). *Pet loss: Grief waves – 6 tips.*https://www.foreverinmyheartpetlosscounselling.com.au/pet-loss-counsellor-grief-counselling-australia-melbourne/pet-loss-grief-waves-6-tipshttps://www.foreverinmyheartpetlosscounselling.com.au/pet-loss-counsellor-grief-counselling-australia-melbourne/pet-loss-grief-waves-6-tips

- Funeral Basics. (n.d.). *10 family-focused pet remembrance ideas.*https://www.funeralbasics.org/10-family-focused-pet-remembrance-ideas/https://www.funeralbasics.org/10-family-focused-pet-remembrance-ideas/

- Funeral.com. (n.d.). *Phantom sounds after pet loss: Why you hear them and how to cope with sensory grief at home.*https://funeral.com/blogs/the-journal/phantom-sounds-after-pet-loss-why-you-hear-them-how-to-cope-with-sensory-grief-at-homehttps://funeral.com/blogs/the-journal/phantom-sounds-after-pet-loss-why-you-hear-them-how-to-cope-with-sensory-grief-at-home

- Funeral.com. (n.d.). *What to say when someone loses a pet.*https://funeral.com/blogs/the-journal/what-to-say-when-someone-loses-a-pet-texts-cards-workplace-scripts-and-what-not-to-sayhttps://funeral.com/blogs/the-journal/what-to-say-when-someone-loses-a-pet-texts-cards-workplace-scripts-and-what-not-to-say

- Galena Animal. (2025). *DIY pet memorials: Guide for pet owners.*https://galenaanimal.com/diy-pet-memorials/https://galenaanimal.com/diy-pet-memorials/

- Gentle Journey AZ. (n.d.). *Dealing with guilt after pet euthanasia.*https://www.gentlejourneyaz.com/blog/in-home-euthanasia/dealing-with-guilt-after-pet-euthanasiahttps://www.gentlejourneyaz.com/blog/in-home-euthanasia/dealing-with-guilt-after-pet-euthanasia

- HelpGuide.org. (n.d.). *Coping with losing a pet.*https://www.helpguide.org/mental-health/grief/coping-with-losing-a-pethttps://www.helpguide.org/mental-health/grief/coping-with-losing-a-pet

- Lap of Love. (n.d.). *Overcoming guilt after losing your*

*pet.*https://www.lapoflove.com/blog/pet-loss-support/ overcoming-guilt-after-losing-your-pethttps:// www.lapoflove.com/blog/pet-loss-support/overcoming-guilt- after-losing-your-pet

- Lap of Love. (n.d.). *Pet loss support services.* https:// www.lapoflove.com/our-services/pet-loss-supporthttps:// www.lapoflove.com/our-services/pet-loss-support

- Memories.net. (n.d.). *9 easy steps to creating an online pet memorial.* https://memories.net/blog/online-pet- memorialhttps://memories.net/blog/online-pet-memorial

- National Geographic. (n.d.). *The "Rainbow Bridge" has comforted millions of pet parents.* https:// www.nationalgeographic.com/animals/article/rainbow-bridge- poem-pet-death-mourning-origin-revealedhttps:// www.nationalgeographic.com/animals/article/rainbow-bridge- poem-pet-death-mourning-origin-revealed

- NPR. (2023). *8 creative and loving ways to honor a pet's memory.* https://www.npr.org/2023/09/27/1198493559/ loving-ways-to-honor-pets-memory-write-obit-grow-garden- dedicate-dayhttps://www.npr.org/2023/09/27/1198493559/ loving-ways-to-honor-pets-memory-write-obit-grow-garden- dedicate-day

- Pet Ventures. (n.d.). *10 meaningful cat memorial ideas.* https:// petventuresbook.com/blogs/blog/gone-but-never- forgotten-10-meaningful-cat-memorial-ideashttps:// petventuresbook.com/blogs/blog/gone-but-never- forgotten-10-meaningful-cat-memorial-ideas

- Pets Plus Us. (n.d.). *Paw print keepsake & ornament: DIY dog* *or cat.*https://www.petsplusus.com/blog/diy-paw-print-keepsakehttps://www.petsplusus.com/blog/diy-paw-print-keepsake

- Psychology Today. (2017). *7 self-care essentials while grieving the death of a pet.*https://www.psychologytoday.com/us/blog/animal-attachment/201702/7-self-care-essentials-while-grieving-the-death-of-a-pethttps://www.psychologytoday.com/us/blog/animal-attachment/201702/7-self-care-essentials-while-grieving-the-death-of-a-pet

- Psychology Today. (2022). *Why do we grieve losing a pet so deeply?*https://www.psychologytoday.com/us/blog/heartstrings/202211/why-do-we-grieve-losing-a-pet-so-deeplyhttps://www.psychologytoday.com/us/blog/heartstrings/202211/why-do-we-grieve-losing-a-pet-so-deeply

- PubMed Central. (n.d.). *A study on the attachment to pets among owners of cats and dogs.*https://pmc.ncbi.nlm.nih.gov/articles/PMC11718770/https://pmc.ncbi.nlm.nih.gov/articles/PMC11718770/

- Rip Companion. (n.d.). *Living pet memorials: How to plant a garden or tree in memory of your pet.*https://www.ripcompanion.com/blog/20-living-pet-memorials-how-to-plant-a-garden-or-tree-in-memory-of-your-pet/https://www.ripcompanion.com/blog/20-living-pet-memorials-how-to-plant-a-garden-or-tree-in-memory-of-your-pet/

- The Skinny Pig NYC. (2020). *A goodbye letter to Bobo, my beloved cat for 14 years.*https://www.theskinnypignyc.com/2020/12/a-goodbye-letter-to-bobo-my-beloved-cat-for-14-years/https://

www.theskinnypignyc.com/2020/12/a-goodbye-letter-to-bobo-my-beloved-cat-for-14-years/

- Tiny Buddha. (n.d.). *What I learned about love and grief when I lost my cats.*https://tinybuddha.com/blog/what-i-learned-about-love-and-grief-when-i-lost-my-cats/https://tinybuddha.com/blog/what-i-learned-about-love-and-grief-when-i-lost-my-cats/

- Tiny Pet Memories. (2017). *Go slowly: When to keep and give away pet possessions.*https://tinypetmemories.com/2017/08/07/dont-rush-slowly-give-pet-possessions-away/https://tinypetmemories.com/2017/08/07/dont-rush-slowly-give-pet-possessions-away/

- Two Hearts Pet Loss Center. (n.d.). *Navigating pet loss through mindfulness.*https://twoheartspetlosscenter.com/navigating-pet-loss-through-mindfulness-creating-a-rhythm-for-healing/https://twoheartspetlosscenter.com/navigating-pet-loss-through-mindfulness-creating-a-rhythm-for-healing/

- VCA Animal Hospitals. (n.d.). *Helping your grieving pet.*https://vcahospitals.com/know-your-pet/helping-your-grieving-pethttps://vcahospitals.com/know-your-pet/helping-your-grieving-pet